Allyn & Bacon
Casebook Series
Sexual Abuse

Edited by

Jerry L. Johnson

Grand Valley State University

George Grant, Jr.

Grand Valley State University

PEARSON

Boston • New York • San Francisco
Mexico City • Montreal • Toronto • London • Madrid • Munich • Paris
Hong Kong • Singapore • Tokyo • Cape Town • Sydney

Senior Series Editor: *Pat Quinlin*
Series Editorial Assistant: *Nakeesha Warner*
Marketing Manager: *Laura Lee Manley*
Production Editor: *Won McIntosh*
Editorial Production Service: *Stratford*
Composition Buyer: *Linda Cox*
Manufacturing Buyer: *JoAnne Sweeney*
Electronic Composition: *Stratford*
Cover Administrator: *Elena Sidorova*

For related titles and support materials, visit our online catalog at
www.ablongman.com

To obtain permission(s) to use material from this work, please submit a written
request to Allyn and Bacon, Permissions Department, 75 Arlington Street, Boston,
MA 02116 or fax your request to 617-848-7320.

Between the time website information is gathered and then published, it is not
unusual for some sites to have closed. Also, the transcription of URLs can result
in typographical errors. The publisher would appreciate notification where these
errors occur so that they may be corrected in subsequent editions.

Library of Congress Cataloging-in-Publication Data

Sexual abuse / edited by Jerry L. Johnson, George Grant, Jr.
    p. cm. — (Allyn & Bacon casebook series)
  ISBN 0-205-48186-8
  1. Sex crimes. 2. Social work education. I. Johnson, Jerry L.,
  II. Grant, George, Jr.

HV6556.S427 2007
364.15'3—dc22

                    2006023982

Printed in the United States of America

10 9 8 7 6 5 4 3 2 1   11 10 09 08 07 06

*To all of those who have helped,
advised, supported, criticized, and forgiven.
You know who you are.*

Jerry L. Johnson

*To my wife Beverly, who inspires and supports me
in all my endeavors. In loving memory
of my father and mother George and Dorothy Grant.*

George Grant Jr.

Contents

Preface

This text offers students the chance to study the work of experienced social workers as they practice in various settings with sexually abuse clients and their families. As graduate and undergraduate social work educators, we (the editors) have struggled to find quality practice materials that translate well into a classroom setting. Over the years, we have used case materials from our practice careers, professionally produced audio-visuals, and tried other casebooks. While each had its advantages, we could not find a vehicle that allowed students to study the work of experienced practitioner's that took students beyond the belief that practice is a technical endeavor that involves finding "correct" interventions to solve client problems.

We want our students to study and analyze how experienced practitioners think about practice and how they struggle to resolve ethical dilemmas and make treatment decisions that meet the needs of their clientele. We want students to review and challenge the work of others in a way that allows them to understand what comprises important practice decisions with real clients in real practice settings. That is, we want classroom materials that allow students entry into the minds of experienced practitioners.

Goals of the Casebook

This Casebook focuses on practice with sexually abused clients in a variety of settings and from diverse backgrounds. Our goal is to provide students with an experience that:

1. Provides personal and intimate glimpses into the thinking and actions of experienced practitioners as they work with clients. In each case, students may demonstrate their understanding of the cases and how and/or why the authors approached their case in the manner presented.

2. Provides a vehicle to evaluate the process, ideas, and methods used by the authors. We also wanted to provide students a chance to present their ideas about how they would have worked differently with the same case.
3. Affords students the opportunity to use evidence-based practice findings (Gibbs, 2003; Cournoyer, 2004) as part of the case review and planning process. We challenge students to base practice judgments and case planning exercises on current practice evidence available through library and/or electronic searches, and practice wisdom gained through consultation and personal experience when the evidence is conflicted or lacking.

To meet our goals, the cases we included in this text focus on the practice *process*, specifically client engagement, assessment, and the resultant clinical process, including the inevitable ethical dilemmas that consistently arise in daily practice. We aim to demonstrate the technical and artistic elements involved in developing and managing the various simultaneous processes involved in practice. While we recognize the difficulty of presenting process information (circular) in a linear medium (book), we have tried to do the best job possible towards this end.

To achieve our goals, we include four in-depth case studies in this text. In each case study, authors guide students through the complete practice process, from initial contact to client termination and practice evaluation. Focusing on multi-systemic client life history (see Chapter 1), students get a detailed look into the life history and presentation of each client. Throughout each case, we challenge students to participate through a series of in-depth and thoughtful questions and assignments. Each case asks students to develop a written narrative assessment, diagnostic statement, and a treatment and intervention plan. We have used these cases as in-class exercises, small group discussions, the basis for semester-long term papers, and as comprehensive final examinations that integrate multifaceted student learning in practice courses across the curriculum.

Rationale

As former practitioners, we chose the cases carefully. Therefore, the cases in this text focus on the process (thinking, planning, and decision-making) of social work practice and not necessarily on techniques or outcome. Do not be fooled by this statement. Obviously, we believe in successful client outcome based, at least in part, on the use of evidence-based practice methods and current research findings. As important as this is, it is not our focus here—with good reason.

Our experience suggests that instructive process occurs in cases that have successful and unsuccessful outcome. In fact, we often learned more from unsuccessful cases than successful cases. We learned the most when events did not play out as planned. While some of the cases terminated successfully, others were not. This is not a commentary on the author or the author's skill level. Everyone has cases (sometimes too many) that do not turn out as planned. We chose cases based on one simple criterion: did it provide the best possible hope for practice education. We asked authors to teach practice by considering cases that were interesting and difficult, regardless of outcome. We did not want the Casebook to become simply a vehicle to promote practice brilliance.

Mostly, we wanted this text to differ from other casebooks, because we were unsatisfied with casebooks as teaching tools. As part of the process of planning our casebooks, we reviewed other casebooks and discussed with our graduate and undergraduate students approaches that best facilitated learning in the classroom. We discovered that many students were also dissatisfied with a casebook approach to education, for a variety of reasons. Below, we briefly address what our students told us about casebooks in general.

1. *Linear Presentation.* One of the most significant problems involves case presentation. Generally, this involves two issues: linearity and brevity. Most written case studies give students the impression that practice actually proceeds smoothly, orderly, and in a sequential manner. These cases often leave students believing—or expecting—that clinical decisions are made beforehand and that practice normally proceed as planned. In other words, students often enter the field believing that casework follows an *"A, leads to B, leads to C, leads to clients living happily ever after"* approach.

   Experienced practitioners know better. In over 40 years of combined social work practice in a variety of different settings, we have learned—often the "hard way"—that the opposite is true. We rarely, if ever, had a case proceed sequentially, whether our client is an individual, couple, family, group, community, or classroom. That is, the process of engagement (including culturally competence), assessment, treatment planning, intervention, and follow-up occur in a circular manner, rooted in the client's social, physical, and cultural context, and includes consideration of the practitioner, their organization, and the laws and policies that affect and/or determine the boundaries of social work practice and treatment funding.

   Practice evolves in discontinuous cycles over time, including time-limited treatments mandated by the managed care system. Therefore, real-life clinical practice—just as in all developing human relationships—seems to consistently require stops and starts, take wrong-turns, and even, in some cases, require "do-overs." While the goal of competent practice is to facilitate an orderly helping process that includes planned change (Timberlake, Farber, & Sabatino, 2002), practice, as an orderly process, is more often a goal (or a myth) than planned certainty. Given the linearity of case presentations discussed above, readers are often left without an appreciation or understanding of practice as process.

   Additionally, many of the case presentation texts we reviewed provided "hard" client data and asking students to develop treatment plans based on this data. Yet, as any experienced practitioner knows, the difficulty in practice occurs during engagement and data collection. The usual case approach often overlooks this important element of practice. While a book format limits process writing, we believe that the case format we devised here brings student closer to the "real thing."

2. *Little focus on client engagement.* As we like to remind students, there are two words in the title of our profession: social and work. In order for the "work" to be successful, students must learn to master the "social"—primarily, client engagement and relationship building. Social work practice is relationship based (Saleebey, 2002) and, from our perspective, relies more on the processes involved in relationship building and client engagement than technical intervention skills (Johnson, 2004). Successful practice is often rooted more in the ability of practitioners to develop open and trusting relationships with client(s) than on their ability to employ specific methods of intervention (Johnson, 2004).

Yet, this critically important element of practice often goes understated or ignored. Some texts even assume that engagement skills somehow exist before learning about practice. We find this true in casebooks and primary practice texts as well. When it is discussed, engagement and relationship building is presented as a technical process that also proceeds in linear fashion. Our experience with students, employees, and practitioner/trainees over the last two decades suggests that it is wrong to assume that students and/or practitioners have competent engagement or relationship building skills. From our perspective, developing a professional relationship that involves trust and openness, where clients feel safe to dialogue about the most intimate and sometimes embarrassing events in their lives, is the primary responsibility of the practitioner, and often spells the difference between positive and negative client outcome (Johnson, 2004; Miller & Rollnick, 2002; Harper & Lantz, 1996). Hence, each case presentation tries to provide a sense of this difficult and often elusive process and some of the ways that the authors overcame challenges to the culturally competent client engagement process.

Target Audience

Our target audience for this text, and the others in the series, are advanced undergraduate as well as foundation and advanced graduate students in social work and other helping disciplines. We have tested our approach with students at several different points in their education. We find that the casebooks can be used as:

- An adjunct learning tool for undergraduates preparing for or already involved in their field practicum.
- Practice education and training for foundation-level graduate students in practice theory and/or methods courses.
- An adjunct learning tool for second-year graduate students in field practicum.
- An adjunct learning tool for undergraduate and/or graduate students in any practice courses pertaining to specific populations.

While we are social work educators, we believe the casebooks will be useful in social work and other disciplines in the human services, including counseling psychology, counseling, mental health, psychology, and specialty disciplines such as marriage and family therapy, substance abuse, and mental health degree or certificate programs. Any educational or training program designed to prepare students to work with clients in a helping capacity may find the casebooks useful as a learning tool.

Structure of Cases

We organized the case studies to maximize critical thinking, the use of professional literature, evidenced-based practice knowledge, and classroom discussion in the learning process. At various points throughout each case, we comment on issues and/or dilemmas highlighted by the case. Our comments always end with a series of questions designed to focus student learning by calling on their ability to find and evaluate evidence from the professional literature and through classroom discussion. We ask students to collect evidence on different sides of an issue, evaluate that evidence, and develop a professional position that they can defend in writing and/or discussion with other students in the classroom or seminar setting.

We hope that you find the cases and our format as instructive and helpful in your courses, as we have in ours. We have field tested our format in courses at our university, finding that students respond well to the length, depth, and rigor of the case presentations. Universally, students report that the case materials were an important part of their overall learning process.

Organization of the Text

We organized this text to maximize its utility in any course. Chapter 1 provides an overview of the Advanced Multi-Systemic (AMS) practice approach. We provide this as one potential organizing tool for students to use while reading and evaluating the subsequent cases. This chapter offers students an organized and systematic framework to use when analyzing cases and/or formulating narrative assessments, treatment, and intervention plans. Our intent is to provide a helpful tool, not make a political statement about the efficacy or popularity of one practice framework versus others. In fact, we invite faculty and students to apply whatever practice framework they wish when working the cases.

In Chapter 2, author *Jan Wrenn, ACSW, MSW*, presents her work with Kate, a 24 year old newly married woman and mother who begins having marital problems and depression. Later in therapy, the author discovers that her client was sexually abused as a child.

In Chapter 3, *Cathy Simmons, MSW, Med., BCD* presents a case involving an adult male sexual abuse survivor whose life experiences prepared him for successful therapy. In a chapter called Austin, readers get to see how the author uses systems interventions to help an individual overcome a traumatic childhood of sexual abuse.

In Chapter 4, *Leslie Menhart, MSW, CSW* offers an interesting case involving Dani, an harshly abused adolescent female who enters residential treatment after conviction as a sex offender. Menhart takes readers through a difficult case that involves multi-systemic involvement of other practitioners and teamwork.

The final chapter, Mary, presents *Cathy Simmons', MSW, Med., BCD* work with an alcohol dependent woman with multiple, co-occurring disorders. During treatment, Simmons discovers that Mary was also a sexual abuse victim as a child and adult.

Acknowledgments

We would like to thank the contributors to this text, Jan Wrenn, Cathy Simmons (twice), and Leslie Menhart for their willingness to allow their work to be challenged and discussed in a public venue. We would also like to thank Patricia Quinlin and the people at Allyn and Bacon for their faith in the Casebook Series and in our ability to manage fourteen manuscripts in a short time. Additionally, we have to thank all of our students and student assistants that served as "guinea pigs" for our case studies. Their willingness to provide honest feedback contributes mightily to this series.

Jerry L. Johnson—I want to thank my wife, Cheryl, for her support and willingness to give me the time and encouragement to write and edit. I also owe a debt of gratitude to my dear friends Hope, Zelda, and Amaris, for being there when I need them the most.

George Grant, Jr.—I want to thank Dean Rodney Mulder and Dr. Elaine Schott for their insight, encouragement, and support during this process. I also thank Dr. Julius Franks and Professor Daniel Groce for their intellectual discourse and unwavering support.

Contributors

The Editors

Jerry L. Johnson, Ph.D., MSW is an Associate Professor in the School of Social Work at Grand Valley State University in Grand Rapids Michigan. He received his MSW from Grand Valley State University and his Ph.D. in sociology from Western Michigan University. Johnson has been in social work for more than 20 years as a practitioner, administrator, consultant, and teacher. He received two Fulbright Scholarship awards to Albania in 1998-99 and 2000-01. In addition, Johnson serves in various consulting capacities in countries such as Albania and Armenia. He is the author of two previous books, *Crossing Borders—Confronting History: Intercultural Adjustment in a Post-Cold War World* (2000, Rowan and Littlefield) and *Fundamentals of Substance Abuse Practice* (2004, Wadsworth Brooks/Cole). With George Grant, Jr., he co-edits the *Allyn & Bacon Casebook Series* that includes casebooks in Substance Abuse, Mental Health, Foster Care, Adoption, Medical Social Work, Community Practice, and Domestic Violence.

George Grant, Jr., Ph.D., MSW is an Associate Professor in the School of Social Work at Grand Valley State University in Grand Rapids, Michigan where he also serves as the Director of the MSW Program. Grant, Jr., also serves as the Director of Grand Valley State university's BSW Program. He received his MSW from Grand Valley State University and Ph.D. in sociology from Western Michigan University. Grant, Jr., has a long and distinguished career as practitioner, administrator, consultant, teacher, and trainer in social work, primarily in fields dedicated to Child Welfare. With Jerry L. Johnson, he co-edits the *Allyn & Bacon Casebook Series* that includes casebooks in Substance Abuse, Mental Health, Foster Care, Adoption, Medical Social Work, Community Practice, and Domestic Violence.

Jan Wrenn, ACSW, MSW, has taught in the social work department at Andrews University since 1996, teaching both BSW and MSW students. She also served as the BSW Program Director for three years. Prior to teaching, Jan worked in an outpatient clinical social work position, where she counseled children, adolescents, adults, couples and families. She received her MSW from The University of Michigan

Cathy Simmons, MSW, Med., BCD is a clinical social worker and a Ph.D. Candidate at the University of Texas at Arlington. For the past 9 years, she has worked as an Air Force social worker in both the crisis intervention and domestic violence arenas. As a crisis interventionist she has responded to over 2-dozen critical incidents and either been a part of or been the team leader of crisis intervention teams in three different states and three different countries. Additionally, she has run domestic violence treatment programs in Kunsan, South Korea, Oahu, Hawaii, and Misawa, Japan. Currently, she is working on her dissertation titled "Male and Female Trauma Narratives: Differences and Similarities" and working as both an adjunct professor at UTA and a clinical social worker at Sheppard Air Force Base, Texas.

Lesley Menhart, MSW, CSW has been practicing in the field of social work since 1993. Her clinical work has focused primarily in the areas of working with adult and child survivors of sexual abuse as well as adult and child sexual perpetrators. She has also held various supervisory roles in the social work field. She is a member of the adjunct faculty of the University of Phoenix, West Michigan Campus. She has presented at various West Michigan professional trainings on issues related to sexual abuse. She was also a national presenter at the 2002 national convention of forensic counselors.

Bibliography

Cournoyer, B. R. (2004). *The evidence-based social work skills book*. Boston: Allyn & Bacon.
Germain, C. B., & Gitterman, A. (1996). *The life model of social work practice* (2nd ed.). New York: Columbia University Press.
Gibbs, L. E. (2003). *Evidence-based practice for the helping professions: A practical guide with integrated multimedia*. Pacific Grove, CA: Brooks/Cole.

Harper, K. V., & Lantz, J. (1996). *Cross-cultural practice: Social work practice with diverse populations*. Chicago: Lyceum Books.

Johnson, J. L. (2004). *Fundamentals of substance abuse practice*. Pacific Grove, CA: Brooks/Cole.

Miller, W. R., & Rollnick, S. (2002). *Motivational interviewing: Preparing people to change addictive behavior* (2nd ed.). New York: Guilford Press.

Saleebey, D. (2002). *The strengths perspective in social work practice* (3rd ed.). Boston: Allyn & Bacon.

Timberlake, E. M., Farber, M. Z., & Sabatino, C. A. (2002). *The general method of social work practice: McMahon's generalist perspective* (4th ed.). Boston: Allyn & Bacon.

A Multi-Systemic Approach
to Practice

Jerry L. Johnson and George Grant, Jr.

This is a practice-oriented text, designed to build practice skills with individuals, families, and groups. We intend to provide you the opportunity to study the process involved in treating real cases from the caseloads of experienced practitioners. Unlike other casebooks, we include fewer cases, but provide substantially more detail in hopes of providing a realistic look into the thinking, planning, and approach of the practitioners/authors. We challenge you to study the author's thinking and methods to understand their approach and then use critical thinking skills and the knowledge you have gained in your education and practice to propose alternative ways of treating the same clients. In other words, what would your course of action be if you were the primary practitioner responsible for these cases? Our hope is that this text provides a worthwhile and rigorous experience studying real cases as they progressed in practice.

Before proceeding to the cases, we include this chapter as an introduction to the Advanced Multi-Systemic (AMS) practice perspective. We decided to present this introduction with two primary goals in mind. First, we want you to use the information contained in this chapter to help assess and analyze the cases in this text. You will have the opportunity to complete a multi-systemic assessment, diagnoses, treatment, and intervention plan for each case. This chapter will provide the theoretical and practical basis for this exercise. Second, we hope you find that AMS makes conceptualizing cases clearer in your practice environment. We do not suggest that AMS is the only way, or even the best way for every practitioner to conceptualize cases. We simply know, through experience, that AMS is an effective way to think about practice with client-systems of all sizes and configurations. While there are many approaches to practice, AMS offers an effective way to place clinical decisions in the context of client lives and experiences, making engagement and treatment productive for clients and practitioners.

Advanced Multi-Systemic (AMS) Practice

Sociological Roots

> Whether the point of interest is a great power state or a minor literary mood, a family, a prison, and a creed—these are the kinds of questions the best social analysts have asked. They are the intellectual pivots of classic studies of (person) in society—and they are the questions inevitably raised by any mind possessing the sociological imagination. For that imagination is the capacity to shift from one perspective to another—from the political to the psychological; from examination of a single family to comparative assessment of the national budgets of the world; from the theological school to the military establishment; from considerations of an oil industry to studies of contemporary poetry. It is the capacity to range from the most impersonal and remote transformations to the most intimate features of the human self—and see the relations between the two. Back of its use is always the urge to know the social and historical meaning of the individual in the society and in the period in which he (or she) has his quality and his (or her) being (Mills, 1959, p. 7; parentheses added).

Above, sociologist C. Wright Mills provided a seminal description of the sociological imagination. As it turns out, Mills' sociological imagination is also an apt description of AMS. Mills believed that linking people's "private troubles" to "public issues" (p. 2) was the most effective way to understand people and their issues, by placing them in historical context. It forces investigators to contextualize individuals, families, and communities in the framework of the larger social, political, economic, and historical environments in which they live. Ironically, this is also the goal of social work practice (Germain & Gitterman, 1996; Longres, 2000). Going further, Mills (1959) stated:

> We have come to know that every individual lives, from one generation to the next, in some society; the he (or she) lives out a biography, and that he (or she) lives it out within some historical sequence. By the fact of his (or her) living he (or she) contributes, however minutely, to the shaping of this society and to the course of its history, even as he (or she) is made by society and by its historical push and shove (p. 6).

Again, Mills was not speaking as a social worker. He was an influential sociologist, speaking about a method of social research. In *The Sociological Imagination*, Mills (1959) proposed this as a method to understand the links between people, their daily lives, and their multi-systemic environment. Yet, while laying the theoretical groundwork for social research, Mills also provided the theoretical foundation for an effective approach to social work practice. We find four relevant points in *The Sociological Imagination* that translate directly to social work practice.

1. It is crucial to recognize the relationships between people's personal issues and strengths (private troubles) and the issues (political, economic, social, historical, and legal) and strengths of the multi-systemic environment (public issues)

in which people live daily and across their lifespan. A multi-systemic understanding includes recognizing and integrating issues and strengths at the micro (individual, family, extended kin, etc.), mezzo (local community), and macro (state, region, national, and international policy, laws, political, economic, and social) levels during client engagement, assessment, treatment, follow-up, and evaluation of practice. This is true whether your client is an individual, family, small group, or community association. This requirement does not change, only the point where investigation begins.

2. This depth of understanding (by social workers and especially, clients) can lead to change in people's lives. We speak here about second-order change, or, significant change that makes a long-term difference in people's lives; change that helps people view themselves differently in relationship to their world. This level of change becomes possible when people, alone or in groups, make multi-systemic links in a way that makes sense to them (Freire, 1993). In other words, clients become "empowered" to change when they understand their life in the context of their world, and realize that they have previously unforeseen or unimagined choices in how they live, think, believe, and act.

3. Any assessment and/or clinical diagnoses that exclude multi-systemic links do not provide a holistic picture of people's lives, their troubles, and/or strengths. In sociology, this leads to a reductionist view of people and society, while in social work it reduces the likelihood that services will be provided (or received by clients) in a way that addresses client problems and utilizes client strengths in a meaningful way. The opportunity for change is reduced whenever client life history is overlooked because it does not fit, or is not called for, in a practitioner's preferred method of helping, or because of shortcuts many people believe are needed in a managed care environment. One cannot learn too much about their clients, their lives, and their attitudes, beliefs, and values as it relates to the private troubles presented in treatment.

4. Inherent in AMS and foundational to achieving all that was discussed above relies on practitioners being able to rapidly develop rapport with clients and client systems that leads to engagement in treatment or action. In this text, client engagement

> . . . occurs when you develop, in collaboration with clients, a trusting and open professional relationship that promotes hope and presents viable prospects for change. Successful engagement occurs when you create a social context in which vulnerable people (who often hold jaded attitudes toward helping professionals) can share their innermost feelings, as well as their most embarrassing and shameful behavior with you, a *total stranger* (Johnson, 2004, p. 93; emphasis in original).

AMS Overview

First, we should define two important terms that comprise AMS. Understanding these terms is important, because they provide the foundation for understanding the language and concepts used throughout the remainder of this chapter.

1. **Advanced.** According to Derezotes (2000), "the most advanced theory is also the most inclusive" (p. viii). AMS is advanced because it is inclusive. It requires responsible practitioners, in positions of responsibility (perhaps as solo practitioners) to acquire a depth of knowledge, skills, and self-awareness that allows for an inclusive application of knowledge acquired in the areas of human behavior in the social environment, social welfare policy, social research and practice evaluation, and multiple practice methods and approaches in service of clients and client systems of various sizes, types, and configurations.

   AMS practitioners are expected to have the most inclusive preparation possible, "both the broad generalist base of knowledge, skills, and values and an in-depth proficiency in practice . . . with selected social work methods and populations" (Derezotes, 2000, p. xii). Hence, advanced practitioners are well trained and with in-depth knowledge, are often in positions of being responsible for clients as primary practitioners. They are afforded the responsibility for engaging, assessing, intervening, and evaluating practice, ensuring that clients are ethically treated in a way that is culturally competent and respectful of their client's worldview. In other words, AMS practitioners develop the knowledge, skills, and values needed to be leaders in their organizations, communities, the social work profession, and especially in the treatment of their clients. The remainder of this chapter explains why AMS is an advanced approach to practice.

2. **Multi-Systemic.** From the earliest moments in their education, social workers learn a systems perspective that emphasizes the connectedness between people and their problems to the complex interrelationships that exist in their client's world (Timberlake, Farber, & Sabatino, 2002). To explain these connections, systems theory emphasizes three important concepts: wholeness, relationships, and homeostasis. Wholeness refers to the notion that the various parts or elements (subsystem) of a system that interact to form a whole that best describe the system in question. This concept asserts that no system can be understood or explained unless the connectedness of the subsystems to the whole are understood or explained. In other words, the whole is greater than the sum of its parts. Moreover, systems theory also posits that change in one subsystem will affect change in the system as a whole.

In terms of systems theory, relationship refers to the patterns of interaction and overall structures that exist within and between subsystems. The nature of these relationships is more important than the system itself. That is, when trying to understand or explain a system (individual, family, or organization, etc.) how subsystems connect through relationships, the characteristics of the relationships between subsystems, and how the subsystems interact provide clues to understanding the system as a whole. Hence, the application of systems theory is primarily based on understanding relationships. As someone once said about systems theory, in systems problems occur between people and subsystems (relationships), not "in" them. People's internal problems relate to the nature of the relationships in the systems where they live and interact.

Homeostasis refers to the notion that most living systems work to maintain and preserve the existing system, or the status quo. For example, family members often assume roles that serve to protect and maintain family stability, often at the expense of "needed" change. The same can be said for organizations, groups, or community associations. The natural tendency toward homeostasis in systems represents what we call the "dilemma of change" (Johnson, 2004). This can best be described as the apparent conflict, or what appears to be client resistance or lack of motivation, that often occurs when clients approach moments of significant change. Systems of all types and configurations struggle with the dilemma of change: should they change to the unknown or remain the same, even if the status quo is unhealthy or unproductive? Put differently, systems strive for stability, even at the expense of health and well being of individual members and/or the system itself.

What do we mean then, by the term *multi-systemic*? Clients (individuals, families, communities, etc) are systems that interact with a number of different systems simultaneously. These systems exist and interact at multiple levels, ranging from the micro level (individual and families), the mezzo level (local community, institutions, organizations, the practitioner and their agency, etc.), to the macro level (culture, laws and policy, politics, oppression and discrimination, international events, etc.). How these various systems come together, interact, and adapt, along with the relationships that exist within and between each system work together to comprise the "whole" that is the client, or client-system.

In practice, the client (individual, couple, family, community, etc.) is not the "system," but one of many interacting subsystems in a maze of other subsystems constantly interacting to create the system—the client plus elements from multiple subsystems at each level. It would be a mistake to view the client as the whole system. They are but one facet of a multi-dimensional and multi-level system comprised of the client and various other subsystems at the micro, mezzo, and macro levels.

Therefore, the term *multi-systemic* refers to the nature of a system comprised of the various multi-level subsystems described above. A multi-systemic perspective recognizes that clients or client systems are *one part or subsystem* in relationship with other subsystemic influences occurring on different levels. This level of understanding—the system as the whole produced through multi-systemic subsystem interactions—is the main unit of investigation for practice. As stated above, it is narrow to consider the client as a functioning independent system with peripheral involvement with other systems existing outside of their intimate world. These issues and relationships work together to help shape and mold the client who in turn, shapes and molds their relationship to the other subsystems. Yet, the person-of-the-client is but one part of the system in question during practice.

AMS provides an organized framework for gathering, conceptualizing, and analyzing multi-systemic client data and for proceeding with the helping process. It defines the difference between social work and other disciplines in the helping professions at the level of theory and practice. How, you ask? Unlike other professional disciplines that tend to focus on one or a few domains (i.e., psychology, medicine, etc.), AMS provides a comprehensive and holistic "picture" of clients or client-systems in the context of their environment by considering information about multiple personal and systemic domains simultaneously. Moreover, practitioners can use AMS to address clients and client systems of all sizes and configurations. That is, this approach works as well with communities or international projects as it does with individuals or families seeking therapy.

Resting on the generalist foundation taught in all Council on Social Work Education (CSWE) accredited undergraduate and foundation-level graduate programs, AMS requires practitioners to contextualize client issues in the context of the multiple interactions that occur between the client/client-system and the social, economic, legal, political and physical environment in which the client lives. It is a unifying perspective based in the client's life, history, and culture that guides the process of collecting and analyzing client life information and intervening to promote personal choice through a comprehensive, multi-systemic framework. Beginning with culturally competent client engagement, a comprehensive multi-systemic assessment points toward a holistically based treatment plan that requires practitioners to select and utilize appropriate practice theories, models, and methods—or combinations thereof—that best fit the client's unique circumstances and needs.

AMS is not a practice theory, model, or method itself. It is a perspective or framework for conceptualizing client-systems. It relies on the practitioner's ability to use a variety of theories, models, and methods, and to incorporate knowledge from human behavior, social policy, research/evaluation, and practice into their routine approach with clients. For example, an AMS practitioner will have the skills to apply different approaches to individual treatment (client-centered, cognitive-behavioral, etc.), family treatment (structural, narrative, Bowenian, etc.), work with couples, in groups, arrange for specialized care if needed, and, as an advocate on behalf of their client. It may also require practitioners to treat clients in a multi-modal approach (i.e., individual and group treatments simultaneously). Additionally, AMS practitioners can work with community groups and organizations at the local regional, or national level.

Practitioners not only must know how to apply different approaches, but also how to determine, primarily through the early engagement and assessment process, which theory, model, or approach (direct or indirect, for example) would work best for a particular client. Hence, successful practice using AMS relies heavily on the practitioner's ability to competently engage and multi-systemically assess client problems and strengths. Practitioners must simultaneously develop a sense of their client's personal interaction and relationship style—especially related to how they relate to authority figures—when determining which approach would best suit the client. For example, a reserved, quiet, or thoughtful client or someone who lacks assertiveness may not be well served by a directive, confrontational approach, regardless of the practitioner's preference. Moreover, AMS practitioners rely on professional practice research and outcome studies to help determine which approach or intervention package might work best for particular clients and/or client systems.

AMS expects practitioners to know how to find and evaluate practice research in their practice areas or specialties.

Elements of the Advanced Multi-Systemic Approach to Social Work Practice

The advanced multi-systemic approach entails the following seven distinct, yet integrated elements of theory and practice. Each is explained below.

Ecological-Systems Perspective

One important sub-category of systems therapy for social work is the ecological systems perspective. This perspective combines important concepts from the science of ecology and general systems theory into a way of viewing client problems and strengths in social work practice. In recent years, it has become the prevailing perspective for social work practice (Miley, O'Melia, & DuBois, 2004). The ecological systems perspective—sometimes referred to as the ecosystems perspective—is a useful metaphor for guiding social workers as they think about cases (Germain & Gitterman, 1980).

Ecology focuses on how subsystems work together and adapt. In ecology, adaptation is "a dynamic process between people and their environments as people grow, achieve competence, and make contributions to others" (Greif, 1986, p. 225). Insight from ecology leads to an analysis of how people fit within their environment and what adaptations are made in the fit between people and their environments. Problems develop as a function of inadequate or improper adaptation or fit between people and their environments.

General systems theory focuses on how human systems interact. It focuses specifically on how people grow, survive, change, and achieve stability or instability in the complex world of multiple systemic interactions (Miley, O'Melia, & DuBois, 2004). General systems theory has contributed significantly to the growth of the family therapy field and to how social workers understand their clients.

Together, ecology and general systems theory evolved into what social workers know as the ecological systems perspective. The ecological systems perspective provides a systemic framework for understanding the many ways that persons and environments interact. Accordingly, individuals and their individual circumstances can be understood in the context of these interactions. The ecological systems perspective provides an important part of the foundation for AMS. Miley, O'Melia, and DuBois (2004) provide an excellent summary of the ecological systems perspective. They suggest that it,

1. Presents a dynamic view of human beings as systems interaction in context.
2. Emphasizes the significance of human system interactions.
3. Traces how human behavior and interaction develop over time in response to internal and external forces.

4. Describes current behavior as an adaptive fit of "persons in situations."
5. Conceptualizes all interaction as adaptive or logical in context.
6. Reveals multiple options for change within persons, their social groups, and in their social and physical environments (p. 33).

Social Constructionism

To maintain AMS as an inclusive practice approach, we need to build on the ecological systems perspective by including ideas derived from social constructionism. Social constructionism builds on the ecological systems perspective by introducing ideas about how people define themselves and their environment. Social constructionism also, by definition, introduces the role of culture in the meaning people give to themselves and other systems in their multi-systemic environments. The ecological systems perspective discusses relationships at the systemic level. Social constructionism introduces meaning and value into the equation, allowing for a deeper understanding and appreciation of the nature of multi-systemic relationships and adaptations.

Usually, people assume that reality is something "out there" that hits them in the face, something that independently exists, and people must learn to "deal with it." Social constructionism posits something different. Evolving as a critique of the "one reality" belief system, social constructionism points out that the world is comprised of multiple realities. People define their own reality and then live within those definitions. Accordingly, the definition of reality will be different for everyone. Hence, social constructionism deals primarily with meaning, or the systemic processes by which people come to define themselves in their social world. As sociologist W.I. Thomas said, in what has become known as the Thomas Theorem, "If people define situations as real, they are real in their consequences."

For example, some people believe that they can influence the way computerized slot machines pay-out winnings by the way they sit, the feeling they get from the machine as they look at it in the casino, by the clothes they are wearing, or by how they trigger the machine, either by pushing the button or pulling the handle. Likewise, many athletes believe that a particular article of clothing, a routine for getting dressed, and/or a certain pregame meal dictates the quality of their athletic prowess that day.

Illogical to most people, the belief that they can influence a computerized machine, that the machine emits feelings, or that an article of clothing dictates athletic prowess is real to some people. For these people, their beliefs influence the way they live. Perhaps you have ideas or "superstitions" that you believe influences how your life goes on a particular day. This is a common occurrence. These people are not necessarily out-of-touch with objective reality. While people may know, at some level, that slot machines pay according to preset, computerized odds or that athletic prowess has nothing to do with dressing routines, the belief systems continue. What dictates the behavior and beliefs discussed above or in daily "superstitions" have nothing to do with objective reality and everything to do with people's subjective reality. Subjective reality—or a person's learned definition of the situation—overrides objectivity and helps determine how people behave and/or what they believe.

While these examples may be simplistic, according to social constructionism, the same processes influence everyone—always. In practice, understanding that people's behavior does not depend on the objective existence of something, but on their subjective interpretation of it, is crucial to effective application of AMS. This knowledge is most helpful during client engagement. If practitioners remember that practice is about understanding people's perceptions and not objective reality, they reduce the likelihood that clients will feel misunderstood, there will be fewer disagreements, and easier to avoid the trap of defining normal behavior as client resistance or a diagnosable mental disorder. This perspective contributes to a professional relationship based in the client's life and belief systems, is consistent with their worldview, and one that is culturally appropriate for the client. Being mindful that the definitions people learn from their culture underlies not only what they do but also what they perceive, feel, and think places practitioners on the correct path to "start where the client is." Social constructionism emphasizes the cultural uniqueness of each client and/or client-system and the need to understand each client and/or client-system in their own context and belief systems, not the practitioner's context or belief systems.

Social constructionism also posits that different people attribute different meaning to the same events, because the interactional contexts and the way individuals interpret these contexts are different for everyone, even within the same family or community. One cannot assume that people raised in the same family will define their social world similarly. Individuals, in the context of their environments, derive meaning through a complex process of individual interpretation. This is how siblings from the same family can be so different, almost as if they did not grow up in the same family. For example, the sound of gunfire in the middle of the night may be frightening or normal, depending upon where a person resides and what is routine and accepted in their specific environment. Moreover, simply because some members of a family or community understand nightly gunfire as normal does not mean that others in the same family or community will feel the same.

Additionally, social constructionism examines how people construct meaning with language and established or evolving cultural beliefs. For example, alcohol consumption is defined as problematic depending upon how the concept of "alcohol problem" is socially constructed in specific environments. Clients from so-called drinking cultures may define drinking six alcoholic drinks daily as normal, while someone from a different cultural background may see this level of consumption as problematic. One of the authors worked in Russia and found an issue that demonstrates this point explicitly. Colleagues in Russia stated rather emphatically that consuming one "bottle" (approximately a U.S. pint) of vodka per day was acceptable and normal. People that consume more than one bottle per day were defined as having a drinking problem. The same level of consumption in the United States would be considered by most as clear evidence of problem drinking.

Biopsychosocial Perspective

Alone, the ecological systems perspective, even with the addition of social constructionism, does not provide the basis for the holistic understanding required by AMS. While it provides a multi-systemic lens, the ecological systems perspective focuses mostly on externals. That is, how people interact and adapt to their environments and how environments interact and adapt to people. Yet, much of what practitioners consider "clinical" focuses on "internals" or human psychological and emotional functioning. Therefore, the ecological systems perspective provides only one part of the holistic picture required by the advanced multi-systemic approach. By adding the biopsychosocial perspective, practitioners can consider the internal workings of human beings to help explain how external and internal subsystems interact.

What is the biopsychosocial perspective? It is a theoretical perspective that considers how human biological, psychological, and social-functioning subsystems interact to account for how people live in their environment. Similar to social systems, human beings are also multidimensional systems comprised of multiple subsystems constantly interacting in its environment, the human body. The biopsychosocial perspective applies multi-systemic thinking to individual human beings.

Several elements comprise the biopsychosocial perspective. Longres (2000) identifies two dimensions of individual functioning, the biophysical, and the psychological; subdividing the psychological into three sub-dimensions: the cognitive, affective, and behavioral. Elsewhere, we added the spiritual/existential dimension to this conception (Johnson, 2004). Understanding how the biological, psychological, spiritual and existential, and social subsystems interact is instrumental in developing an appreciation of how individuals influence and are influenced by their social systemic environments. Realizing that each of these dimensions interacts with external social and environmental systems allow practitioners to enlarge their frame of reference, leading to a more holistic multi-systemic view of clients and client-systems.

Strengths/Empowerment Perspective

Over the last few years, the strengths perspective has emerged as an important part of social work theory and practice. The strengths perspective represents a significant change in how social workers conceptualize clients and client-systems. According to Saleebey (2002), it is "a versatile practice approach, relying heavily on ingenuity and creativity . . . Rather than focusing on problems, your eye turns toward possibility" (p. 1). Strengths-based practitioners believe in the power of possibility and hope in helping people overcome problems by focusing on, locating, and supporting existing personal or systemic strengths and resiliencies. The strengths perspective is based on the belief that people, regardless of the severity of their problems, have the capabilities and resources to play an active role in helping solve their own problems. The practitioner's role is to engage clients in a way that unleashes these capabilities and resources toward solving problems and changing lives.

Empowerment

Any discussion of strengths-based approaches must also consider empowerment as an instrumental element of the approach. Empowerment, as a term in social work, has evolved over the years. We choose a definition of empowerment that focuses on power; internal, interpersonal, and environmental (Parsons, Gutierrez, & Cox, 1998). According to Parsons, Gutierrez, and Cox (1998),

> In its most positive sense, power is (1) the ability to influence the course of one's life, (2) an expression of self worth, (3) the capacity to work with others to control aspects of public life, and (4) access to the mechanisms of public decision making. When used negatively, though, it can also block opportunities for stigmatized groups, exclude others and their concerns from decision-making, and be a way to control others (p. 8).

Hence, empowerment in practice is a process (Parsons, Gutierrez, and Cox, 1998) firmly grounded in ecological systems and strength-based approaches that focus on gaining power by individuals, families, groups, organizations, or communities. It is based on two related assumptions: (1) all human beings are potentially competent, even in extremely challenging situations, and (2) all human beings are subject to various degrees of powerlessness (Cox & Parsons, 1994, p. 17) and oppression (Freire, 1993). People internalize their sense of powerlessness and oppression in a way that their definition of self in the world is limited, often eliminating any notion that they can act in their own behalf in a positive manner.

An empowerment approach makes practical connections between power and powerlessness. It illuminates how these factors interact to influence clients in their daily life. Empowerment is not achieved through a single intervention, nor is it something that can be "done" to another. Empowerment does not occur through neglect or by simply giving responsibility for their lives and well-being to the poor or troubled, allowing these people to be "free" from government regulation, support, or professional assistance. In other words, empowerment of disenfranchised groups does not occur simply by dismantling systems (such as the welfare system) to allow these groups or individuals to take responsibility for themselves. Hence, empowerment does not preclude helping.

Consistent with our definition, empowerment develops through the approach taken toward helping, not the act of helping itself. Empowerment is a sense of gained or regained power that someone attains in their life that provides the foundation for change in the short term, and stimulates belief in their ability to positively influence their lives over the long term. Empowerment occurs as a function of the long-term approach of the practitioner and the professional relationship developed between practitioner and client. One cannot provide an empowering context through a constant focus on problems, deficits, inadequacies, negative labeling, and dependency.

The Power of Choice

Choice is an instrumental part of strengths-based and empowerment approaches, by recognizing that people, because of inherent strengths and capabilities, can make informed choices about their lives, just like people who are not clients. Practitioners work toward offering people choices about how they define their lives and problems, the extent to which they want to address their problems, and the means or mechanisms through which change should occur. Clients become active and instrumental partners in the helping process. They are not passive vessels, waiting for practitioners to "change them" through some crafty intervention or technique.

We are not talking about the false choices sometimes given to clients by practitioners. For example, clients with substance abuse problems are often told that they must either abstain or leave treatment. Most practitioners ignore or use as evidence of denial, client requests to attempt so-called controlled use. If practitioners were interested in offering true choice, they would work with these clients toward their controlled-drinking goal in an effort to reduce the potential harm that may result from their use of substances (Johnson, 2004; van Wormer & Davis, 2003), even if the practitioner believes that controlled-drinking is not possible. Abstinence would become the goal only when their clients choose to include it as a goal.

Client Engagement as Cultural Competence

Empowerment (choice) occurs through a process of culturally competent client engagement, created by identifying strengths, generating dialogue targeted at revealing the extent of people's oppression (Freire, 1993) and respecting their right to make informed choices in their lives. Accordingly, empowerment is the, "transformation from individual and collective powerlessness to personal, political, and cultural power" (GlenMaye, 1998, p. 29), through a strengths-based relationship with a professional helper.

Successful application of AMS requires the ability to engage clients in open and trusting professional relationships. The skills needed to engage clients from different backgrounds and with different personal and cultural histories are what drives practice; what determines the difference between successful and unsuccessful practice. Advanced client engagement skills allow the practitioner to elicit in-depth, multi-systemic information in a dialogue between client and practitioner (Johnson, 2004), providing the foundation for strengths-based client empowerment leading to change.

Earlier, we defined client engagement as a mutual process occurring between clients and practitioners in a professional context, created by practitioners. In other words, creating the professional space and open atmosphere that allows engagement to flourish is the primary responsibility of the practitioner, not the client. Practitioners must have the skills and knowledge to adjust their approach toward specific clients and the client's cultural context and not *vice versa*. Clients do not adjust to us and our beliefs, values, and practices—we adjust to them. When that occurs, the foundation exists for client engagement. By definition, relationships of this nature must be performed in a culturally competent manner. Yet, what does this mean?

Over the last two decades, social work and other helping professions have been concerned with cultural competence in practice (Fong, 2001). Beginning in the late

1970's the professional literature has been replete with ideas, definitions, and practice models designed to increase cultural awareness and promote culturally appropriate practice methods. Yet, despite the attention given to the issue, there remains confusion about how to define and teach culturally competent practice.

Structural and Historical Systems of Oppression: Who Holds the Power?

Often embedded in laws, policies, and social institutions are oppressive influences such as racism, sexism, homophobia, and classism, to name a few. These structural issues play a significant role in the lives of clients (through maltreatment and discrimination) and in social work practice. How people are treated (or how they internalize historical treatment of self, family, friends, and/or ancestors) shapes how they believe, think, and act in the present. Oppression affects how they perceive that others feel about them, how they view the world and their place in it, and how receptive they are to professional service providers. Therefore, culturally competent practice must consider the impact of structural systems of oppression and injustice on clients, their problems, strengths, and potential for change.

Oppression is a by-product of socially constructed notions of power, privilege, control, and hierarchies of difference. As stated above, it is created and maintained by differences in power. By definition, those who have power can force people to abide by the rules, standards, and actions the powerful deem worthwhile, mandatory, or acceptable. Those who hold power can enforce particular worldviews; deny equal access and opportunity to housing, employment, or healthcare; define right and wrong, normal and abnormal; and imprison, confine, and/or commit physical, emotional, or mental violence against the powerless (McLaren, 1995; Freire, 1993). Most importantly, power permits the holder to "set the very terms of power" (Appleby, 2001, p. 37). It defines the interaction between the oppressed and the oppressor, and between the social worker and client.

Social institutions and practices are developed and maintained by the dominant culture to meet *its* needs and maintain *its* power. Everything and everybody is judged and classified accordingly. Even when the majority culture develops programs or engages in helping activities, these efforts will not include measures that threaten the dominant group's position at the top of the social hierarchy (Freire, 1993). For example, Kozol (1991) wrote eloquently about how public schools fail by design, while Freire (1993) wrote about how state welfare and private charity provide short-term assistance while ensuring that there are not enough resources to lift people permanently out of poverty.

Oppression is neither an academic nor a theoretical consideration; it is not a faded relic of a bygone era. Racism did not end with the civil rights movement, and sexism was not eradicated by the feminist movement. Understanding how systems of oppression work in people's lives is of paramount importance for every individual and family seeking professional help, including those who belong to the *same* race, gender, and class as the practitioner. No two individuals, regardless of their personal demographics, experience the world in the same way. Often, clients are treated ineffectively by professional helpers who mistakenly believe that people who look or act the same will experience the world in similar ways. These workers base their assumptions about clients on stereotypic descriptions of culture, lifestyle, beliefs and practices. They take group-level data (i.e., many African American adolescents join gangs because of broken families and poverty) and assume that *all* African American teenagers are gang members from single-parent families. Social work values and ethics demand a higher standard, one that compels us to go beyond stereotypes. Our job is to discover, understand, and utilize personal differences in the assessment and treatment process to benefit clients, not use differences as a way of limiting clients' potential for health and well-being.

We cannot accurately assess or treat people without considering the effects of oppression related to race, ethnicity, culture, sexual preference, gender, or physical/emotional status. We need to understand how oppression influences our clients' beliefs about problems and potential approaches to problem-solving, and how it determines what kind of support they can expect to receive if they decide to seek help. For example, despite the widely held belief that chemical dependency is an equal opportunity disease (Gordon, 1993), it is clear that some people are more vulnerable than others. While some of the general themes of chemical dependency may appear universal, each client is unique. That is, an individual's dependency results from personal behavior, culture (including the history of one's culture), past experiences, and family interacting with larger social systems that provide opportunities or imposes limits on the individual (Johnson, 2000).

Systems of oppression ensure unequal access to resources for certain individuals, families, and communities. However, while all oppressed people are similar in that they lack the power to define their place in the social hierarchy, oppression based on race, gender, sexual orientation, class, and other social factors is expressed in a variety of ways. Learning about cultural nuances is important in client assessment, treatment planning, and treatment (Lum, 1999). According to Pinderhughes (1989), there is no such thing as culture-free service delivery. Cultural differences between clients and social workers in terms of values, norms, beliefs, attitudes, lifestyles, and life opportunities affect every aspect of practice.

What is Culture?

Many different concepts of culture are used in social work, sociology, and anthropology. Smelser (1992) considers culture a "system of patterned values, meanings, and beliefs that give cognitive structure to the world, provide a basis for coordinating and controlling human interactions, and constitute a link as the system is transmitted from one generation to another" (p. 11). Geertz (1973) regarded culture as simultaneously a product of and a guide to people searching for organized categories and interpretations that provide a meaningful experiential link to their social life. Building upon these two ideas, in this book we abide by the following definition of culture proposed elsewhere (Johnson, 2000):

Culture is historical, bound up in traditions and practices passed through generations; memories of events—real or imagined—that define a people and their worldview. (Culture) is viewed as collective subjectivity, or a way of life adopted by a community that ultimately defines their worldview (p. 121).

Consistent with this definition, the collective subjectivities called culture are pervasive forces in the way people interact, believe, think, feel, and act in their social world. Culture plays a significant role in shaping how people view the world. As a historical force, in part built on ideas, definitions, and events passed through generations, culture also defines people's level of social acceptance by the wider community; shapes how people live, think, and act; and influences how people perceive that others feel about them and how they view the world and their place in it. Thus, it is impossible to understand a client without grasping their cultural foundations.

Cultural Competence

As stated earlier, over the years many different ideas and definitions of what constitutes culturally competent practice have developed, as indicated by the growth of the professional literature since the late 1970's. To date, focus has primarily been placed in two areas: (1) the need for practitioners to be aware or their own cultural beliefs, ideas, and identities leading to cultural sensitivity, and (2) learning factual and descriptive information about various ethnic and racial groups based mostly on group-level survey data and analyses. Fong (2001) suggests that culture is often considered "tangential" to individual functioning and not central to the client's functioning (p. 5).

To address this issue, Fong (2001) builds on Lum's (1999) culturally competent practice model that focuses on four areas: (1) cultural awareness, (2) knowledge acquisition, (3) skill development, and (4) inductive learning. Besides inductive learning, Lum's model places focuses mainly on practitioners in perpetual self-awareness, gaining knowledge about cultures, and skill building. While these are important ideas for cultural competence, Fong (2001) calls for a shift in thinking and practice, "to provide a culturally competent service focused solely on the client rather than the social worker and what he or she brings to the awareness of ethnicity" (p. 5). Fong (2001) suggests an "extension" (p. 6) of Lum's model by turning the focus of each of the four elements away from the practitioner toward the client. For example, cultural awareness changes from a practitioner focus to, "the social worker's understanding and the identification of the critical cultural values important to the client system and to themselves" (p. 6). This change allows Fong (2001) to remain consistent with the stated definition of culturally competent practice, insisting that practitioners,

. . . operating from an empowerment, strengths, and ecological framework, provide services, conduct assessments, and implement interventions that are reflective of the clients' cultural values and norms, congruent with their natural help-seeking behaviors, and inclusive of existing indigenous solutions (p. 1).

While we agree with the idea that "to be culturally competent is to know the cultural values of the client system and to use them in planning and implementing services" (Fong, 2001, p. 6), we want to make this shift the main point of a culturally competent model of client engagement. That is, beyond what should or must occur, we believe that professional education and training must focus on the skills of culturally competent client engagement that are necessary to make this happen; a model that places individual client cultural information at the center of practice. We agree with Fong (2001) that having culturally sensitive or culturally aware practitioners is not nearly enough. Practitioner self-awareness and knowledge of different cultures does not constitute cultural competence. We strive to find a method for reaching this worthy goal.

The central issue revolves around practitioners participating in inductive learning and the skills of grounded theory. In other words, regardless of practitioner beliefs, awarenesses, or sensitivities, their job is to learn about and understand their client's world, and "ground" their theory of practice in the cultural context of their client. They develop a unique theory of human behavior in a multi-systemic context for every client. Culturally competent client engagement does not happen by assessing the extent to which client lives "fit" within existing theory and knowledge about reality, most of which is middle-class and Eurocentric at its core. Cultural competence (Johnson, 2004),

> . . . *begins* with learning about different cultures, races, personal circumstances, and structural mechanisms of oppression. It *occurs* when practitioners master the interpersonal skills needed to move beyond general descriptions of a specific culture or race to learn specific individual, family, group, or community interpretations of culture, ethnicity, and race. The culturally competent practitioner knows that within each culture are individually interpreted and practiced thoughts, beliefs, and behaviors that may or may not be consistent with group-level information. That is, there is tremendous diversity within groups, as well as between them. Individuals are unique unto themselves, not simply interchangeable members of a specific culture, ethnicity, or race who naturally abide by the group-level norms often taught on graduate and undergraduate courses on human diversity (p. 105).

Culturally competent client engagement revolves around the practitioner's ability to create a relationship, through the professional use of self, based in true dialogue (Freire, 1993; Johnson, 2004). We define dialogue as, "a joint endeavor, developed between people (in this case, practitioner and client) that move clients from their current state of hopelessness to a more hopeful, motivated position in their world (Johnson, 2004, p. 97). Elsewhere (Johnson, 2004), we detailed a model of culturally competent engagement based on Freire's (1993; 1972) definitions of oppression, communication, dialogue, practitioner self-work, and the ability to exhibit worldview respect, hope, humility, trust, and empathy."

To investigate culture in a competent manner is to take a comprehensive look into people's worldview—to discover what they believe about the world and their place in it. It goes beyond race and ethnicity (although these are important issues) into how culture determines thoughts, feelings, and behaviors in daily life. This includes what culture says about people's problems; culturally appropriate strengths and resources; the impact of gender on these issues; and what it means to seek professional help (Leigh, 1998).

The larger questions to be answered are how clients uniquely and individually interpret their culture; how their beliefs, attitudes, and behaviors are shaped by that interpretation, and, how these cultural beliefs and practices affect daily life and determine lifestyle in the context of the larger community. Additionally, based on their cultural membership, beliefs, and practices, practitioners need to discover the potential and real barriers faced by clients in the world. For many clients, because they are part of non-majority cultures expose them to issues generated by social systems of oppression such as racism, sexism, homophobia, and ethnocentrism that expose them to limitations and barriers that others do not face.

What is the value of culturally competent client engagement? Helping clients discuss their attitudes, beliefs, and behaviors in the context of their culture—including their religious or spiritual belief systems—offers valuable information about their worldview, sense of social and spiritual connection, and/or practical involvement in their social world. Moreover, establishing connections between their unique interpretation of their culture and their daily life provides vital clues about people's belief systems, attitudes, expectations (social construction of reality), and explanation of behaviors that cannot be understood outside the context of their socially constructed interpretation of culture.

A Cautionary Note

It is easy to remember to ask about culture when clients are obviously different (i.e., different races, countries of origin, etc.). However, many practitioners forgo cultural investigation with clients they consider to have the same cultural background as the practitioner. For example, the search for differences between European-Americans with Christian beliefs—if the social worker shares these characteristics—gets lost in mutual assumptions, based on the misguided belief that there are no important differences between them. The same is often true when clients and practitioners come from the same racial, cultural, or lifestyle backgrounds (i.e., African American practitioner and client, Gay practitioner and gay client, etc.). Culturally competent practice means that practitioners are always interested in people's individual interpretation of their culture and their subjective definitions of reality, whether potential differences are readily apparent or not. Practitioners must be diligent to explore culture with clients who appear to be from the same background as the practitioner, just as they would with people who are obviously from different cultural, racial, ethnic, or religious backgrounds.

Multiple Theories & Methods

No single theory, model, or method is best suited to meet the needs of all clients (Miley, O'Melia, & DuBois, 2004). Consistent with this statement, one of the hallmarks of

AMS is the expectation that practitioners must determine which theory, model, or method will best suit a particular client. Choosing from a range of approaches and interventions, AMS practitioners develop the skills and abilities to: (1) based on the client's life, history, culture, and style, determine which treatment approach (theory and/or method) would best suit their needs and achieve the desired outcome, (2) which modality or modalities (individual, family, group treatment, etc.) will best meet the need of their clients, and (3) conduct treatment according to their informed clinical decisions.

Over the last 20 years or so, graduate social work education has trended toward practice specialization through concentration-based curricula. Many graduate schools of social work build on the generalist foundation by insisting that students focus on learning specific practice models or theories (disease, cognitive-behavioral, psychoanalysis, etc.) and/or specific practice methods (individual, family, group, etc.), often at the exclusion of other methods or models. For example, students often enter the field intent on doing therapy with individuals say, from a cognitive-behavioral approach only.

This trend encourages practitioners to believe that one approach or theory best represents the "Truth." Truth, in this sense, is the belief that one theory or approach works best for most people, most of the time. It helps create a practice scenario that leads practitioners to use their chosen approach with every client they treat. Therefore, practice becomes a process of the practitioner forcing clients to adjust to the practitioner's beliefs and expectations about the nature of problems, the course of treatment, and definition of positive versus negative outcomes. From this perspective, what is best for clients are determined by what the practitioner believes is best, not on what clients believe is in their best interest.

Some practitioners take their belief in the Truth of a particular theory or method to extremes. They believe that one model or theory works best for all people, all the time. We found this to be common in the family therapy field, whereby some true believers insist that everyone needs family therapy—so that is all they offer. What's worse is that many of these same practitioners know and use only one particular family therapy theory and model. The "true believer" approach can cause problems, especially for clients. For example, when clients do not respond to treatment, instead of looking to other approaches, true believers simply prescribe more of the method that did not work in the first place. If a more intensive application of the method does not work, then the client's "lack of readiness" for treatment, resistance, or denial becomes the culprit. These practitioners usually give little thought to their practice approach or personal style and its impact on client "readiness" for treatment. They fail to examine the role their personal style, beliefs, attitudes, and practices have in creating the context that led to clients not succeeding in treatment.

Each practice theory and model has a relatively unique way of defining client problems, practitioner method and approach, interventions, and what constitutes successful outcome. For practitioners to believe that one theory or model is true, even if only for most people, they must believe in the universality of problems, methods and approaches, interventions, and successful outcome criteria. This contradicts the definition of theory. While being far from a concrete representation of the truth, a theory is a set of myths, expectations, guesses, and conjectures about what might be true (Best & Kellner, 1991). A theory is hypothetical; a set of ideas and explanations that need proving. No single theory can explain everything. According to Popper (1994), a theory ". . . always remains guesswork, and there is no theory that is not beset with problems" (p. 157). As such, treatment specialization can—although not always— encourage people to believe they have found the Truth where little truth exists.

Practitioners using an AMS perspective come to believe that some element of every established practice model, method, or theory may be helpful. Accordingly, every model, method, or theory can be adapted and used in a multi-systemic practice framework. As an AMS practitioner, one neither accepts any single model fully, nor disregards a model entirely if there is potential for helping a client succeed in a way that is compatible with professional social work values and ethics. These practitioners hone their critical thinking skills (Gambrill, 1997, 1990) and apply them in practice, particularly as it pertains to treatment theories, models, and methods. In the context of evidence-based practice (Cournoyer, 2004; Gibbs, 2003), sharpened critical thinking skills allow practitioners to closely read and evaluate practice theories, research, or case reports to recognize the strengths, weakness, and contradictions in theories, models, and/or policy related to social work practice.

Informed Eclecticism

The goal of AMS related to treatment methods is for practitioners to develop an approach we call *informed eclecticism.* Informed eclecticism allows the use of multiple methods, interventions, and approaches in the context of practice that: (1) is held together by a perspective or approach that provides consistency; that makes practice choices in a way that makes sense in a particular client's life, and (2) is based, whenever possible, on the latest evidence about its efficacy with particular problems and particular clients. While it is often best to rely on empirical evidence, this data is in its infancy. AMS does not preclude the use of informed practice wisdom and personal creativity in developing intervention plans and approaches. It is up to practitioners to ensure that any treatment based in practice wisdom or that is creatively generated be discussed with colleagues, supervisors, or consultants to ensure theoretical consistency and that it fits within the code of professional ethics.

Informed eclecticism is different from the routine definition of eclecticism—the use of whatever theory, model, or method works best for their clients. While this is the goal of AMS practice specifically and social work practice in general (Timberlake, Farber, & Sabatino, 2004), it is an elusive goal indeed. Informed eclecticism often gets lost in a practitioner's quest to find something that "works." According to Gambrill (1997), eclecticism is "the view that we should adopt whatever theories or methodologies is useful in inquiry, no matter what their source and without worry about their consistency" (p. 93). The most important word in Gambrill's statement is "consistency." While there are practitioners who have managed to develop a consistent, organized, and holistic version of informed eclecticism, this is not the norm.

Too often, uninformed eclecticism resembles the following. A practitioner specializes by modality (individual therapy) and uses a variety of modality-specific ideas and practices in their work with clients; changing ideas and tactics when the approach they normally use does not "work." This often leaves the practitioner searching (mostly in vain) for the magic intervention—what "works." Moreover, while uninformed eclectic practitioners use interventions from various "schools," they remain primarily wedded to one modality. Hence, they end up confusing themselves and their clients as they search for the "right" approach, rarely looking beyond their chosen modality, and therefore, never actually looking outside of their self-imposed, theoretical cage.

For example, an uninformed eclectic practitioner specializing in individual therapy may try a cognitive approach, a client-centered approach, a Freudian approach, or a behavioral approach, etc. A family therapy specialist may use a structural, strategic, or solution-focused approach. However, in the end, little changes. These practitioners still believe that their clients need individual or family treatment. They rarely consider potentially useful ideas and tactics taken from different modalities that could be used instead of, or in combination with, an individual or family approach, mostly because they base treatment decisions on their chosen modality.

While informed eclecticism is the goal, most find it difficult to find consistency when trying to work from a variety of models at the same time. The informed eclectic practitioners, through experience and empirical evidence, have a unifying approach that serves as the basis for using different models or methods. What is important, according to clinical outcome research, is the consistency of approach in helping facilitate successful client outcome (Gaston, 1990; Miller & Rollnick, 2002; Harper & Lantz, 1996). Trying to be eclectic makes consistency (and treatment success), quite difficult.

What uninformed eclecticism lacks is the framework needed to gain a holistic and comprehensive understanding of the client in the context of their life, history, and multiple environments that leads naturally to culturally consistent treatment and intervention decisions. AMS, as it is described here, provides such a framework. It is holistic, integrative, ecological, and based in the latest empirical evidence. It is an inclusive framework that bases treatment decisions on a multi-systemic assessment of specific client history and culture. It is designed, whenever possible, to capitalize on client strengths, be consistent with culturally specific help-seeking behavior, and utilize existing or formulated community-based and/or natural support systems in the client's environment.

Defining Multi-Systemic Client Information

In this section we specifically discuss the different dimensions that comprise AMS practice. This is a general look at what constitutes multi-systemic client life information. There are six levels of information that, when integrated into a life history or clients, demonstrates how multiple theories, models, and approaches can be applied to better understand, assess, and treat clients or client-systems. Generally, the six dimensions (biological, psychological, family, religious/spiritual/existential, social/environmental, and macro) encompass range of information needed to complete a comprehensive, multi-systemic assessment, treatment and intervention plan with client-systems of all sizes and configurations.

1. Biological Dimension

AMS practitioners need to understand what some have called the "mind-body connection," or the links between social/emotional, behavioral, and potential biological or genetic issues that may be, at least in part, driving the problems presented by clients in practice. As scientific evidence mounts regarding the biological and genetic sources of personal troubles (i.e., some mental illness, etc.) it grows imperative for well-trained AMS practitioners to apply this knowledge in everyday work with clients (Ginsberg, Nackerud, & Larrison, 2004). The responsibility for understanding biology and physical health goes well beyond those working in direct health care practice settings (i.e., hospital, HIV, or hospice practice settings). Issues pertaining to physical health confront practitioners in all practice settings.

For example, practitioners working in mental health settings are confronted daily with issues pertaining to human biology; the sources and determinants of mental illness, differential uses of psychotropic medication, and often, the role played in client behavior by proper nutrition, appropriate health care, and even physical rest. In foster care and/or family preservation, practitioners also confront the effects of parental abuses (i.e. fetal alcohol syndrome (FAS), medication management, and child/adolescent physical and biological development issues.

Beyond learning about the potential biological or physical determinants of various client troubles, having a keen understanding of the potential physical and health risks associated with various behaviors and/or lifestyles places practitioners in the position of intervening to save lives. For example, practitioners working with substance abusing or chemically dependent clients must understand drug pharmacology—especially drug-mixing—to predict potentially life threatening physical withdrawal effects and/or to prevent intentional or unintentional harm caused by drug overdose (Johnson, 2004).

AMS requires that practitioners keep current with the latest information about human biology, development, genetics, and potential associated health risks facing clients and client-systems in practice. With that knowledge, practitioners can include this information during client assessment, treatment planning, and intervention strategies. It also requires practitioners to know the limits of professional responsibility. That is, social workers are not physicians and should never offer medical advice or guidance that is not supported by properly trained physicians. Therefore, AMS practitioners utilize the appropriate medical professionals as part of assessment, planning and intervention processes with all clients.

2. Psychological/Emotional Dimension

AMS practitioners need a working knowledge of the ways that psychological and emotional functioning are intertwined with clients problems and strengths, how issues from this dimension contribute to the way their client or client-system inter-acts with self and others in their environment, and how their environments influence their psychological and emotional functioning. There are several important skill sets that practitioners must develop to consider issues in this dimension. First, being able to recognize potential problems through a mental screening examination is a skill necessary to all practitioners. Also, having a keen understanding of the *Diagnostic and Statistical Manual of Mental Disorders* (DSM) (American Psychological Asso-ciation, 2000), including the multi-axial diagnostic process, and recognition of the limits of this tool in the overall multi-systemic assessment process is instrumental. Especially critical is the ability to recognize co-occurring disorders (Johnson, 2004). It is also valuable to learn the Person-in-Environment (PIE) assessment system (Karls & Wandrei, 1994a, 1994b), a diagnostic model developed specifically for social workers to incorporate environmental influences.

In addition to understanding how psychology and emotion affects client mood and behavior, AMS practitioners also know how to employ different theories and models used for treating psychological and emotional functioning problems in the context of client's multi-systemic assessment and treatment plan. This includes methods of treating individuals, families and groups. Depending on client's multi-systemic assessment, each of these modalities or some combination of modalities is appropriate for people with problems in this dimension.

3. Family Dimension

The family is the primary source of socialization, modeling, and nurturing of chil-dren. Hence, the family system has a significant impact on people's behavior, and people's behavior has significant impact on the health and well-being of their family system (Johnson, 2004). By integrating a family systems perspective into AMS, prac-titioners will often be able to make sense of behavior attitudes, beliefs, and values that would otherwise be difficult to understand or explain.

For our purposes, a family is defined as a group of people—regardless of their actual blood or legal relationship—whom clients consider to be members of their family (Johnson, 2004). This definition is designed to privilege client's perceptions and subjec-tive construction of reality and avoid disagreements over who is or is not in someone's family. So, if a client refers to a neighbor as "Uncle Joe," then that perception represents their reality. What good would it do to argue otherwise? Just as in client engagement dis-cussed earlier, AMS practitioners seek to understand and embrace their client's unique definition of family, rather than imposing a rigid standard that may not fit their perceived reality. This is especially important when dealing with gay and lesbian clients. The law may not recognize gay or lesbian marriage, but AMS practitioners must, if that is the nature of the client's relationship and consistent with their belief system.

It is important to have a working knowledge of different theories and approaches to assessing and treating families and couples, as well as the ability to construct three-generation genograms to help conceptualize family systems and characterize the relationships that exist within the family system and between the family and its environment. Family treatment requires unique skills, specialized post-graduate training, and regular supervision before a practitioner can master the methods and call themselves a "family therapist." However, the journey toward mastery is well worth it. Family treatment can be among the most effective and meaningful treatment modalities, often used in conjunction with other modalities (individual and/or group treatment), or as the primary treatment method.

4. Religious/Spiritual/Existential Dimension

Practitioners, students, and social work educators are often wary of exploring issues related to religion and spirituality in practice or the classroom. While there are exceptions, this important dimension often goes unexamined. Exploring people's religious beliefs and/or the tenets of their faith, even if they do not appear to have faith of spiritual beliefs, as they pertain to people's subjective definition of self in relation to the world is an important part of AMS practice.

How clients view themselves in relation to others and their world provides an interesting window into the inner-workings of their individual interpretation of culture. The extent that clients have internalized messages (positive, negative, and/or neutral) about their behavior from their faith community or personal spiritual belief systems can lead to an understanding of why people approach their lives and others in the ways they do. Moreover, much can be learned, based on these beliefs, about people's belief in the potential for change, how change occurs, and whom is best suited to help in that change process (if anyone at all), especially as it relates to the many moral and religious messages conveyed about people with problems.

Examination of this dimension goes beyond discovering which church or synagogue clients attend. It is designed to learn how and by what means clients define themselves and their lives in their worlds. What tenets they use to justify their lives, and how these tenets either support their current lives or can be used to help lead them toward change. There is much to be learned about client culture, how people interpret their culture in daily life, and how they view their life in their personal context from an examination of their religious or spiritual beliefs.

Moreover, religious and spiritual belief systems can also be a source of strength and support when considered in treatment plans. For example, while many clients may benefit from attendance at a community support group (i.e., Alcoholics Anonymous, Overeaters Anonymous, etc.) or professional treatment, some will benefit even more from participation in groups and events through local houses of worship. In our experience, many clients unable to succeed in professional treatment or support groups found success through a connection or reconnection with organizations that share their faith, whatever that faith may be.

5. Social/Environmental Dimension

Beyond the individual and family, AMS practitioners look to the client's community, including the physical environment, for important clues to help with engagement, assessment, and intervention planning. People live in communities comprised of three different types: (1) location (neighborhoods, cities, and rural or urban villages), (2) identification (religion, culture, race, etc.), and affiliation (group memberships, subcultures, professional, political/ideological groups, etc.). There are five sub-dimensions that comprise the social/environmental dimension and incorporate the three types of communities listed above (Johnson, 2004). They are:

1. **Local community.** This includes learning about physical environment, living conditions, a person's fit within their community, neighborhoods, where and how people live on a daily basis, and how they believe they are treated and/or accepted by community members and the community's power structure (i.e., the police, etc.).

2. **Cultural context.** This includes learning about clients' larger culture, their individual interpretation of culture, and how it drives or influences their daily life. Also included here is an exploration of histories of oppression and discrimination (individual, family, and community) and a client's sub-cultural group membership (i.e., drug culture, gang culture, etc.).

3. **Social Class.** Often overlooked by practitioners, "information about people's social class is directly related to information about their families, the goodness-of-fit between the person and environment, and the strengths, resources, and/or barriers in their communities" (Johnson, 2004, p. 226). Some believe that no other demographic factor explains so extensively the differences between people and/or groups (Lipsitz, 1997; Davis & Proctor, 1989). Social class represents a combination of income, education, occupation, prestige, and community. It encompasses how these factors affect people's relative wealth and access to power and opportunity (Johnson, 2004).

4. **Social/Relational.** Human beings are social creatures who define themselves in relation to others (Johnson, 2004). Therefore, it is necessary to know something about people's ability to relate to others in their social environment. This investigation includes loved ones, friends, peers, supervisors, teachers, and others that they relate to in their daily life.

5. **Legal History and Involvement.** Obviously, this sub-dimension includes information about involvement with the legal system, by the client, family members, and friends and peers. More than recording a simple demographic history, seek to discover their feelings, attitudes, and beliefs about themselves, their place in the world, and how their brushes with the law fit into or influence their worldview.

6. **Community Resources.** Investigate the nature and availability of organizational support, including the role of social service organizations, politics, and your presence as a social worker in a client's life. For example, can clients find a program to serve their needs, or what does seeing a social worker mean within their community or culture? What are the conditions of the schools and the influence of churches, neighborhood associations, and block clubs? More importantly, what is the prevailing culture of the local environment? Are neighbors supportive

or afraid of each other, and can a client expect to reside in the present situation and receive the support needed to change?

Be sure to include the professional helping system in this sub-dimension. Practitioners, their agencies, and the policies that assist or impede the professional helping process join with client-systems as part of the overall system in treatment. In other words, we must consider ourselves as part of the system—we do not stand outside in objective observation. This includes practitioner qualities and styles, agency policies, broader policies related to specific populations, and reimbursement policies, including managed care. All of these factors routinely influence the extent to which clients receive help, how clients are perceived in the helping system and, in the case of reimbursement policies, the method of treatment clients are eligible to receive regardless of how their multi-systemic assessment turns out.

Familiarity with various theories and models of community provide the keys to understanding the role of the social, physical, political, and economic environment in an individual's life. Community models look at the broader environment and its impact on people. Clients or client systems with issues located in this dimension often respond well to group and family treatment methods. Occasionally, practitioners will be required to intervene at the local neighborhood or community level through organizing efforts and/or personal or political advocacy. For example:

> One author (Johnson) was treating a client in individual and occasional family treatment when it was discovered that the daughter had been molested by a neighbor. The parents had not reported the molestation. I soon learned that this neighbor was rumored to have molested several young girls in the neighborhood and that nobody was willing to report the molestations. I urged my client to organize a neighborhood meeting of all involved parents at her home. I served as the group facilitator for an intense meeting that ultimately built the community support needed to involve law enforcement. Within days, all of the parents in this group met with law enforcement. The perpetrator was arrested, convicted, and sentenced to life imprisonment.

6. Macro Dimension

AMS practitioners do not stop looking for relevant client information at the local level. They also look for clues in the way that macro issues influence clients, their problems, and potential for change. Knowledge of various laws (local, state, and national) are critical, as well as an understanding of how various social policies are interpreted and enforced in a particular client's life. For example, AMS requires an understanding of how child welfare policies affect the life of a chemically dependent mother, how healthcare policy affects a family's decisions about seeking medical treatment for their children, or how local standards of hygiene or cleanliness affect a family's status and acceptance in their community.

Issues to consider at this level also include public sentiment, stereotypes, and mechanisms of oppression that play a significant role in the lives of people who are not Caucasian, male, middle-class (or more affluent) citizens. Racism, classism, homophobia, and sexism, to name a few, are real threats to people who are attempting to live a "normal" life. An AMS practitioner must understand this reality and learn from clients what their individual perceptions are of these mechanisms and how they affect their problems and potential for change. The macro dimension involves issues such as housing, employment, and public support, along with the dynamics of the criminal justice system. For example, if clients have been arrested for domestic violence, what is the chance they will get fair and just legal representation? If they have been convicted and served jail or prison sentences, what are the chances they will have a reasonable chance of finding sufficient employment upon release?

These issues can be addressed in individual, family or group treatments. Often, group treatment is an effective way to address issues clients struggle with at the macro level. Group treatment provides clients a way to address these issues in the context of mutual social support and a sense of belonging, helping them realize that they are not alone in their struggles (Yalom, 1995). AMS practitioners also recognize the need for political advocacy and community organizing methods for clients who present with consistent struggles with issues at the macro level.

Summary

The hallmark of AMS is its reliance on and integration of multi-systemic client information into one, comprehensive assessment, treatment, and intervention plan. It incorporates knowledge, skills, and values from multiple sources, and relies on various sources of knowledge to paint a holistic picture of people's lives, struggles, strengths and resources, and potentials for change. Practitioners need a current working knowledge of human behavior, social systems theories, the latest social research and practice evaluation results, the impact of public laws and policies, as well as the skills and abilities to plan and implement treatment approaches as needed, in a manner consistent with our definition of informed eclecticism.

Many students new to AMS start out confused because the requirements seem so diverse and complicated. However, as you will see in the case presentations to follow, an organized and efficient practitioner who has learned to think and act multi-systemically can gather large amounts of critically important information about a client in a relatively short period. For this to happen, you must have a deep understanding of various theories, models, and practice approaches that address the various systemic levels considered and be willing to accept that no single model is completely right or wrong. It is always easier to latch on to one model and "go with it." However, the goal of practice is not to be correct or to promote your own ease and comfort, but to develop an assessment and treatment plan that is right for each client, whether or not you would ever use it in your own life. Social work practice is not about the social worker, but the client. It is important never to lose sight of this fact.

Bibliography

American Psychiatric Association. (2000). *Diagnostic and statistical manual of mental disorders* (4th ed.). Washington, DC: Author.

Appleby, G. A. (2001). Dynamics of oppression and discrimination. In G. A. Appleby, E. Colon, & J. Hamilton (Eds.), *Diversity, oppression, and social functioning: Person-in-environment assessment and intervention*. Boston: Allyn & Bacon.

Best, S., & Kellner, D. (1991). *Postmodern theory: Critical interrogations*. New York: Guilford Press.

Cournoyer, B. R. (2004). *The evidence-based social work skills book*. Boston: Allyn & Bacon.

Cox, E. O., & Parsons, R. J. (1994). *Empowerment-oriented social work practice with the elderly*. Pacific Grove, CA: Brooks/Cole.

Davis, L. E., & Proctor, E. K. (1989). *Race, gender, and class: Guidelines for practice with individuals, families, and groups*. Englewood Cliffs, NJ: Prentice-Hall.

Derezotes, D. S. (2000). *Advanced generalist social work practice*. Thousand Oaks, CA: Sage.

Fong, R. (2001). Culturally competent social work practice: Past and present. In R. Fong, & S. Furuto (Eds.), *Culturally competent practice: Skills, interventions, and evaluations*. Boston: Allyn & Bacon.

Freire, P. (1993). *Pedagogy of the oppressed*. New York: Continuum.

Gambrill, E. (1997). *Social work practice: A critical thinker's guide*. New York: Oxford University Press.

Gambrill, E. (1990). *Critical thinking in clinical practice*. San Francisco: Jossey-Bass.

Gaston, L. (1990). The concept of the alliance and its role in psychotherapy: Theoretical and empirical considerations. *Psychotherapy, 27*, 143–153.

Geertz, C. (1973). *The interpretation of cultures*. New York: Basic Books.

Germain, C. B., & Gitterman, A. (1980). *The ecological model of social work practice*. New York: Columbia University Press.

Germain, C. B., & Gitterman, A. (1996). *The life model of social work practice* (2nd ed.). New York: Columbia University Press.

Gibbs, L. E. (2003). *Evidence-based practice for the helping professions: A practical guide with integrated multimedia*. Pacific Grove, CA: Brooks/Cole.

Ginsberg, L., Nackerud, L., & Larrison, C. R. (2004). *Human biology for social workers: Development, ecology, genetics, and health*. Boston: Allyn & Bacon.

GlenMaye, L. (1998). Empowerment of women. In L. M. Gutierrez, R. J. Parsons, & E. O. Cox (Eds.), *Empowerment in social work practice: A sourcebook*. Pacific Grove, CA: Brooks/Cole.

Gordon, J. U. (1993). A culturally specific approach to ethnic minority young adults. In E. M. Freeman (Ed.), *Substance abuse treatment: A family systems perspective*. Newbury Park, CA: Sage.

Greif, G. L. (1986). The ecosystems perspective "meets the press." *Social Work, 31*, 225–226.

Harper, K. V., & Lantz, J. (1996). *Cross-cultural practice: Social work practice with diverse populations*. Chicago: Lyceum Books.

Johnson, J. L. (2004). *Fundamentals of substance abuse practice*. Pacific Grove, CA: Brooks/Cole.

Johnson, J. L. (2000). *Crossing borders—confronting history: Intercultural adjustment in a post-Cold War world*. Lanham, MD: University Press of America.

Karls, J., & Wandrei, K. (1994a). *Person-in-environment system: The PIE classification system for functioning problems*. Washington, DC: NASW.

Karls, J., & Wandrei, K. (1994b). *PIE manual: Person-in-environment system: The PIE classification system for social functioning*. Washington, DC: NASW.

Kozol, J. (1991). *Savage inequalities: Children in America's schools*. New York: Crown Publishers.

Leigh, J. W. (1998). *Communicating for cultural competence*. Boston: Allyn & Bacon.

Lipsitz, G. (1997). Class and class consciousness: Teaching about social class in public universities. In A. Kumar (Ed.), *Class issues*. New York: New York University Press.

Longres, J. F. (2000). *Human behavior in the social environment* (3rd ed.). Itasca, IL: F. E. Peacock.

Lum, D. (1999). *Culturally competent practice*. Pacific Grove, CA: Brooks/Cole.

McLaren, P. (1995). *Critical pedagogy and predatory culture: Oppositional politics in a postmodern era*. London: Routledge.

Miley, K. K., O'Melia, M., & DuBois, B. (2004). *Generalist social work practice: An empowerment approach.* Boston: Allyn & Bacon.

Miller, W. R., & Rollnick, S. (2002). *Motivational interviewing: Preparing people to change addictive behavior* (2nd ed.). New York: Guilford Press.

Mills, C. W. (1959). *The sociological imagination.* New York: Oxford University Press.

Parsons, R. J., Gutierrez, L. M., & Cox, E. O. (1998). A model for empowerment practice. In L. M. Gutierrez, R. J. Parsons, & E. O. Cox (Eds.), *Empowerment in social work practice: A sourcebook.* Pacific Grove, CA: Brooks/Cole.

Pinderhughes, E. (1989). *Understanding race, ethnicity, and power.* New York: Free Press.

Popper, K. R. (1994). *The myth of the framework: In defense of science and rationality.* (M. A. Notturno, Ed.). New York: Routledge.

Saleebey, D. (2002). *The strengths perspective in social work practice* (3rd ed.). Boston: Allyn & Bacon.

Smelser, N. J. (1992). Culture: Coherent or incoherent. In R. Munch, & N. J. Smelser (Eds.), *Theory of culture.* Berkeley, CA: University of California Press.

Timberlake, E. M., Farber, M. Z., & Sabatino, C. A. (2002). *The general method of social work practice: McMahon's generalist perspective* (4th ed.). Boston: Allyn & Bacon.

Van Wormer, K., & Davis, D. R. (2003). *Addiction treatment: A strengths perspective.* Pacific Grove, CA: Brooks/Cole.

Yalom, I. (1995). *The theory and practice of group psychotherapy* (4th ed.). New York: Basic Books.

Kate

Jan Wrenn

Meeting Kate

The intake sheet for my next client that day described her as a 24 year-old Caucasian female who said she was "depressed" and having "relationship problems." When I met Mary Kathryn, who preferred Kate, she was a casually dressed blonde woman of average height and weight. She sat in the big rust colored chair in my office, which was the most comfortable one. It had the best view of all my chairs, since it faced a wall of windows overlooking bushes and the sunshine of the bright autumn day. I noticed as she sat down that Kate looked around my office as if to determine whether she liked it. The office has two side chairs with a corner table and a lamp, as well as the soft, rust colored chair, and my desk and chair. I noticed Kate glance for more than a second at my painting of two women walking in a meadow. I could not tell, from her expression if she approved or disapproved. She made no comment about it. I began our first meeting with a bit of informality, asking her if she enjoyed the beautiful fall weather.

Multi-systemic Assessment Information

Kate told me that she is married and has a child, Tim, who is three years-old. She said that she works part-time and finds both her marriage and her role as a mother "challenging." Being a good mother is important to her, she explained, but she finds it stressful, at times, and feels inadequate in this role most of the time. Kate and her husband, Jason, have been married four years. She described this period of her life as "intense." When I asked her to explain, she said that Jason does not understand her "stress level" and that they argue frequently. Kate said there are some sexual difficulties as well, but that she did not want to discuss those at this time.

Kate works part-time at a video store and Jason is a painter. They have been living with her parents since their marriage, because they have not been able to afford to buy a home. Kate said they did not want to rent, instead opting to save money to buy a place of their own. Living with her parents creates stress, but Kate said it is worth the tradeoff because they are able to take care of Tim. I asked her about the stresses of living with her parents and she said her mother is very "controlling." Mother tries telling Kate how to raise her son and always offers unsolicited suggestions about everything from how Kate dresses to how much time she does or does not spend with Tim. Her father is rarely home, working long hours. She said she is more like her father than her mother, adding that her father is much more "laid back" than her mother. Kate explained that she and her mother have always had tension between them and that her father is more accepting. I made a mental note to follow-up on her relationships with her parents at a later session.

My mental status examination of Kate revealed that she was oriented to time, place, person, and situation. Her thought processes were not impaired (for example, she had the ability to think logically and in abstract terms). She denied hallucinations or delusions and I believed her judgment and insight were good, based on her decision to come in for treatment, her taking responsibility for herself, and her level of awareness about her difficulties and their impact on her and on others. Her self image was poor; she made statements about her inability to be successful at anything, saying that she was a "bad wife and mother."

I asked Kate about siblings and she said she has one brother who is five years older than she is. She seemed evasive about her brother. This made me wonder what caused her unwillingness to discuss him or their relationship. I decided not to push it at this point, but to bring it up another time.

Kate said that she had been a quiet, shy, compliant child. Her desire was to make good grades, make her parents happy and proud of her, and not upset anyone. When she was fourteen, however, she began a rebellious phase of her life that included frequent sexual encounters, drugs, alcohol, leaving home for days at a time, and staying out all night at least on weekends, and occasionally during the week. Her parents begged, threatened, took her to see a therapist (which she said was "worthless"), grounded her, and sent her to a strict alternative school for a year. She said nothing made her feel differently, or helped. She changed because she finally got tired of the "scene." When I asked about her current use of drugs and alcohol, Kate said that she has not used drugs since Tim was born. Prior to Tim's birth, she used marijuana once or twice a week and occasionally used cocaine. She and Jason still occasionally go out to a bar on weekends with their friends. However, Kate said she does not drink "as heavily" as she did. I asked her if this was something that was in anyway problematic for her. Kate said that her mother "makes an issue" of it and on a couple of occasions she had not been able to take care of Tim after a drinking binge.

In exploring Kate's health, she said that she has frequent headaches but other than that, she has no health concerns. I asked about her support system. Kate said that her best girlfriend, Casey, is the only one she can truly count on. She has another friend, Ginger, whom she has known since childhood, but has not been as close to her since Ginger's move to another state. She did not mention her parents or Jason in this conversation.

I was curious. According to Kate, neither Jason nor her parents had priority. I wondered about the implications of this statement. I followed up by asking: "Why is that?" She said that Jason had moved out for a few months on two different occasions after fights they had had. "Casey is the only one who is there for me no matter how badly I mess up or how screwed up I feel." Again, I decided to defer the issue of the lack of perceived support from her parents.

Kate told me that her grandmother, whom she had adored and spent a lot of time with as a child, had died a year ago. Kate said that she often felt "alone" since her grandmother's death. She said that her grandmother loved Tim and Kate enjoyed sharing him with her. Kate said that her grandmother was not judgmental of her, of her mothering style, of her lifestyle, or her choices. "Wow, it sounds like your grandmother, like Casey is now, was really there for you," I commented. She nodded and silently cried for a few minutes, without speaking.

It was important for me to explore Kate's strengths. I wanted to do this in a way that validated her but did not diminish her pain or minimize her difficulties. I asked about what she likes to do. Kate said that she enjoys painting and writing poetry. We talked about these hobbies for a while. Kate told me details about how she became interested in them, how old she was when she began, what these hobbies meant to her, and how she felt about them. I commended her on these talents and on her ability to express herself in such creative ways. I also validated her desire and efforts to be a good mother to Tim and to be a good role model for him. We explored what this meant. Kate said that she wants to be "a good person," like her "Grams" was. I also wanted to affirm Kate's efforts and success at giving up drugs because of parenting Tim, which I did.

For Kate, work was a way to earn an income to help support herself, Jason, and Tim. It was not something that she enjoyed or really wanted to do. Her relationships at work were superficial and non-fulfilling. Other community involvement was minimal; she said she does not go to church, does not belong to any clubs or other organizations, and is not involved in any volunteer work or other activities. After completing high school, Kate went to a local college for two years before dropping out. At that time, she had wanted to pursue a career in journalism, possibly working as a newspaper or magazine writer. She gave up those dreams when she lost interest and began thinking of herself as "incapable of completing anything," as she put it. I asked her to explain this. Kate stated that she was not motivated and often felt so "down" that she got involved with drugs and alcohol to "feel better."

Kate indicated on her admissions form that she came in because she felt "depressed" and had "relationship problems." I asked her to tell me about these two concerns. She said that off and on for several years she had been experiencing times when she wanted to stay home in bed and did not have the energy or motivation to do anything. For the past couple of months, she had been feeling this way. However, this time was different somehow from the other times; what scared her about her feelings this time was that she had no interest in anything, including Tim. She was missing work frequently, cried often, felt sad, and had trouble sleeping. I asked if anything had happened to trigger these symptoms and she could not pinpoint any specific incidence, but said, "My life is a wreck." When I asked her to explain what she meant by this, Kate was evasive and added, "I can't do anything right and nobody cares anyway."

I explored what she had done in the past during periods of depression. Kate said that she had been on antidepressants and in therapy, but had always dropped out of therapy and discontinued the medication when she started feeling better. She said that the longest time she had been in therapy was six months. This happened when she teenager and her mother drove her to the appointments and waited there for her. She had been in therapy briefly (a few weeks at the time) several other times, and had been on "four or five" different antidepressants, with the longest period she had taken one being "a few months."

I asked about her relationships and she said her marriage was "ok" at times and "a mess" at other times. She only added that she and Jason argue frequently and do not have a lot of time to spend alone together. Although she said her relationship with her mother was difficult, she was more concerned about her marriage.

Questions

Given the nature of Kate's presenting problems and history to date, answer the following questions before moving ahead with this case.
1. **What is your first hunch regarding Kate and her presenting problem? IS your hunch that Kate is telling her entire history, or do you suspect that she is leaving out important issues?**
2. **What is the next direction of inquiry and assessment? Explore the practice literature to determine what practice models or approaches might work best with Kate and her issues. Based on this inquiry, what information would you need to collect to perform a comprehensive multi-systemic assessment (See Chapter 1)?**
3. **What personal strengths can you locate in addition to those highlighted by the author?**

Initial Session: More Information about Kate

I spent the first session with Kate having four goals/tasks in mind: engagement, assessment, discovering, and emphasizing some of her strengths. I attempted to engage Kate by asking her to tell me her story and why she came for therapy. She said that for the past few weeks she had been feeling "very low" and said that although she had periods like this in the past, this time was worse because she even wanted to avoid spending time with Tim, her three year old. Her best friend, Casey, suggested she needed to get help.

I asked very detailed and specific questions of Kate about her presenting symptoms:

1. How long have you had these symptoms?
2. Did something happen to trigger these symptoms?
3. How much are they interfering with your roles, functioning, and responsibilities?
4. What, if anything, have you done to alleviate the symptoms?
5. Are there times that you do not have the symptoms, and if so, what is going on at those times? What is different about those times?

Kate said she had been feeling "this badly" for the past two months and she could not identify anything that had triggered her feelings. Her symptoms of wanting to isolate herself, feeling sad, crying, and sleep difficulties, were affecting her roles and functioning. She had lost interest in work, often calling in sick, and she had no desire to spend time with Tim. She had been relying on her mother to take care of him. Jason was busy with his work so he had no idea she was feeling as badly as she was. She had been avoiding him too, she admitted. Kate said the only times she did not have symptoms was when she was out drinking with her friend, Casey.

Because of the severity of her symptoms, it was imperative in the initial session to explore suicidal thoughts. Kate said she often thought she would be better off dead, but did not currently have thoughts of suicide. When she was a teenager, Kate said that she had cut her wrist and said she had very much wanted to die. Her boyfriend at the time found her and she spent a few weeks in the hospital. Since that time, Kate said that she had suicidal thoughts from time to time, but no other attempts.

In the initial session, I intentionally focused primarily on her presenting concerns, getting as much detail as I could about those issues. I believe that is important to go slowly, in order not to overwhelm the client or expect her to go further in that session than she wants to go. Exploring strengths is critical, I believe, from the first contact with the client. It is important not to focus just on a problem analysis of the case, looking only at psychopathology, but to highlight the coping and survival skills, as well as other strengths of the client. Equally important is the role that the environment plays in the case, including Kate's support system, her community (work, church, other organizations) and other macro systems which could be affecting her life in a positive or negative way (such as laws or work policies).

At the end of our session, I summarized what we had discussed. Kate and I negotiated two initial goals: alleviating symptoms of depression and looking at specific factors related to dissatisfaction in her marriage. Our goal was to increase satisfaction in her relationship with Jason. We discussed the possibility of Jason joining her for conjoint marital therapy once her depression was under control. I commended her for making the decision to come to the clinic, for her desire to improve her situation, and for her desire to be a good mother. I also stressed her strength in being able to give up drugs in an effort to be a good mother to her son. We discussed agency policies, including confidentiality and an estimated length of therapy (I guessed three months at that time) and agreed to meet weekly, on Tuesday mornings, for the first few weeks.

Questions

Now that the author has presented basic first session information about Kate's life, and before reading on in this case, please perform the following exercises based on your education, experience, the professional literature, and the available best practice evidence. To increase your learning potential, you may want to do this in s small group with other students in your course.

1. Based on the information provided above, construct a three-generation genogram, and eco-map that represents Kate's personal, familial, and environmental circumstances. What further information do you need to complete this exercise? What patterns do these two important graphical assessment tools demonstrate?
2. Based on the same information, construct a list of Kate's issues and strengths, drawing from multi-systemic sources.
3. Write a two- to three-page narrative assessment that encompasses Kate's multi-systemic issues and strengths. Review Chapter 1 if necessary. This narrative should provide a comprehensive and multi-systemic explanation of her life as she prepares to undergo therapy with the author. Importantly, what information is missing? What strategies would you use to gain this information from Kate, given her unique history and personal style?
4. Try identifying a theoretical model or approach that you use to guide your assessment. According to the literature, what other theoretical options are available and how would these options change the nature of your assessment?
5. End by developing multi-axial DSM-IV-TR diagnoses for Kate. Provide a list of client symptoms that you used to justify you diagnostic decisions. What, if any, information was missing that would make this easier?

Reactions to Initial Session and Assessment Information

When I had time at the end of the day to dictate my notes and complete my initial paperwork on Kate, I also had time to reflect on the case. I thought about my goals for that session, engagement, assessment and exploring her strengths. I believed that I had done an adequate job with each of these three goals, but felt better about the assessment and strengths areas than the engagement process.

By asking specific questions about her presenting symptoms, I believed that I could make a diagnosis of major depression. Her symptoms had lasted more than two weeks and were present more often than not. The symptoms she gave me were ones, which are included in DSM-IV-TR for major depression, and since the period of her symptoms also met the criteria, I felt confident in making this diagnosis.

My initial assessment conclusions were that Kate had relied on maladaptive coping behaviors, such as drugs and alcohol, to mask underlying depression and that both the depression and her coping behaviors had contributed to relationship problems as well as to poor self esteem. I had questions about her current motivation level to work in therapy to relieve her depression and relationship concerns, especially since she had in the past dropped out of therapy and discontinued medication without satisfactory resolutions. I felt continued engagement was paramount to any hopes of success in our treatment process.

Each piece of assessment information was important and helpful. The fact that she did not have suicidal thoughts at present was definitely a relief. I also believed that since she seemed to want to be a good mother, and was concerned with her lack of interest at this point in Tim, that these could potentially be motivating forces to work to her advantage.

My questions to myself in analyzing my initial assessment were:

1. Am I guided in my thinking by the relevant information in this case?
2. What other information do I need?
3. Am I avoiding biases of my own in my assumptions?

I did believe that I was attempting to gather and correctly interpret the relevant information in the case. I did not feel that there was countertransference issues involved in our work. Countertransference occurs is when I, as the therapist, react to something about Kate or her situation in a particular way based on something I have experienced in my life. Although I shared a very special relationship with my paternal grandmother who had died a number of years ago, Kate's relationship with her deceased grandmother did not influence my response to her when she mentioned it and subsequently cried.

Follow-up questions on my mind included:

1. Since she has had depression at other times in her life, is there a connection to the other times?
2. How has she coped with her depression in the past?
3. Does her family of origin dynamics contribute to her depression?
4. Why was she evasive about her relationship with her brother?

I wondered if the drugs and alcohol were maladaptive coping behaviors for difficulties Kate was having or had in the past. I wanted to be careful to explore all areas of her life, but at the same time not push her away if there were issues she was not ready or willing to discuss.

Diagnosis

My DSM-IV-TR diagnosis for Kate, as required by the clinic and necessary for reimbursement from her insurance company, was:

Axis I:	Major Depression, recurrent
	Partner relational problem
Axis II:	No diagnosis
Axis III:	None
Axis IV:	Problems with primary support
	Economic problems
Axis V:	Current: 55

I believed Kate had symptoms and appropriate time-frame to meet criteria for major depression. She presented evidence of impairment in both personal and occupational functioning that influenced her condition. My Axis V coding of 55 indicates her current level of functioning. Although she did not have suicidal thoughts, her symptoms were severe enough to cause considerable disruption in her life.

I did not see evidence, in asking mental status exam questions, of mental retardation or personality disorders (Axis II). Her health was good, by her report, and she had not received any medical attention since the birth of Tim three years ago.

The psychosocial and environmental factors (Axis IV), which I believed were important in Kate's life were problems with primary support, including Jason (her husband) as well as her mother. The fact that she and Jason live with her parents and have financial struggles is considered and is coded as economic problems.

Questions

1. **Compare the multi-systemic assessment and diagnoses you developed with the author's assessment and diagnoses. What differences and similarities do you notice? What are the ramifications for treatment demonstrated by the differences between the two assessments? What information would you need to do a better job in this task?**
2. **Based on the assessment and diagnoses you developed, now develop a written, treatment plan that includes short and long term treatment goals. Include what methods of treatment and support you will utilize and/or other levels of care that Kate might require.**
3. **Based on your assessment and treatment plan, what treatment theory, and/or combination of theories do you believe best fits Kate and her reality? Defend your decision.**

Client Engagement

Engaging Kate was not an easy task. I had asked her to tell me her story and why she had come to the clinic. Her explanation was brief, so I asked if I could get some information that I needed for my records. She nodded an ok. I then proceeded to collect her history, attempting to gather as much assessment information as I could. Kate was cooperative, but reluctant with her answers. I could tell she did not trust me and did not want to trust me either. This was a challenge for me; most often in my experience when clients come in for therapy voluntarily, they are willing to talk openly about themselves. In fact, some clients talk non-stop for the first session! Kate was not like them. I was careful not to push her, not wanting to drive her away.

During the session, I used the tools that I regularly use to engage clients. I remained attentive, yet relaxed with my posture. I always sit in my desk chair, but turn to face clients. I make eye contact frequently and a conscious effort to make sure I respond appropriately. That is, I attempt to be consistent with my words, facial, and bodily expressions. I do not want to be dramatic in my response to anything that is said, being careful not to show surprise, disappointment, or embarrassment.

In my practice, I have found that by observing client responses and measuring success of sessions, it is critical that clients feel heard, believed, and accepted for who they are. For this to happen, I MUST remain attentive, alert, and calm. It has helped to train myself to "be present, in the moment" with clients. It is not always easy to put aside the last stressful client, something personal that is on my mind, or to avoid becoming distracted by something about the client. However, in practice, I am convinced that this "presence" is imperative to success. I discuss this in more detail later in the chapter.

It was a welcome relief when, about mid-session, I asked her about times when she has felt like a good mother to Tim. Kate's tone seemed to shift to a slightly more positive one. Using this solution-focused therapy technique of exploring exceptions was helpful at that point in the session. Kate elaborated in more detail than she had previously used about her enjoyment of reading to Tim, playing with him, and taking him to the park. From that point to the end of the initial session, Kate was not as reluctant to share information.

I felt the engagement process had been successful when she agreed, at the end of the session, to come back the following week and to commit to weekly sessions for a few weeks. My next chore would be to continue building our therapeutic relationship so that there would be trust and a willingness on her part to share openly and honestly.

Cultural Competence

After my first session with Kate, I thought about the fact that there were not any relevant pieces of cultural information. However, after learning about the values of her parents and especially her grandmother, I realized that these facts were important to understanding Kate. The family's religious beliefs and practices also played a large part in shaping their reactions to difficulties in life. Kate's family strongly believed that a family keeps their struggles private. They believe that if people pray about struggles, they will be resolved. They also believe that children must respect and obey their parents, above all else.

Her parents' reactions to life struggles convinced her early in childhood that Kate could not share her fears with them. They wanted to believe that their family was "perfect." Therefore, denial of many negative family secrets was part of the family's belief system. This aspect of her family's belief system became a major force in Kate, leading her into some of the maladaptive coping behaviors she struggled with over the years, such as drugs and alcohol.

Questions _____

The author addressed several issue pertaining to cultural competence and engagement in the preceding discussion. Before moving on in the case, are there other issues that you believe must be included in this discussion? If so, explain the issues and discuss the reasons you believe make them important to the case. Moreover,

consider the issues the author included in the discussion. Based on your experience and the professional literature, what is your position on her discussion?

Treatment Planning

At her initial session, Kate said she wanted to relieve her symptoms of depression and focus on strengthening her marriage. She also agreed to three months of therapy. I told her that after a few weeks, we would know if the time-frame would allow her to complete her goals, whether she would need to continue, or renegotiate them. In the first session, I also asked her, and she agreed to see our psychiatrist and take an antidepressant, if prescribed.

Assessment and diagnosis are necessary for formulating a treatment and intervention plan. In my practice, I learned that the time spent in gathering assessment information, reflecting on it, and determining a diagnosis were critical to the formulation of a treatment and intervention plan that would most accurately address the client's concerns. Although an assessment summary is important to treatment and intervention planning, I remind myself that assessment is ongoing; suggesting that the diagnosis and treatment plan may need changing as work progresses.

My Treatment and intervention plan for Kate was:

Goal: Relieve symptoms of depression
Objectives:

1. Report an improvement in the quality and quantity of sleep hours
2. Report an increased interest in usual activities, including the care of Tim
3. Report a decrease in crying and feelings of sadness
4. Report a decrease in feelings of wanting to isolate her from others

Goal: Increase marital satisfaction
Objectives:

1. **Determine** specific problem areas in the marriage
2. Increase frequency of time spent in pleasurable activities with Jason
3. Conjoint therapy to work on areas identified as problematic

Questions

Now that the author has discussed the treatment plan she developed for Kate, compare that treatment plan with the treatment plan you developed for Mary earlier.

1. In what ways does your treatment plan differ from the author's? Please develop an informed critique of the authors plan, and include the reasons you agree or disagree with the author's choices.
2. What do the differences between treatment plans imply for treatment in this case?

Intervention Implementation

After our first session, Kate was scheduled to see a psychiatrist in our clinic. She began taking the antidepressant, Zoloft, within two weeks of our first appointment. After two more weeks, she began seeing dramatic changes in her symptoms of depression. Her sleep patterns improved, the sadness and crying diminished, and she wanted to be with people again. Kate no longer wanted to stay in bed and stay away from work. She also found satisfaction and pleasure in her normal interests, especially in her care of Tim.

During those few weeks, we focused exclusively on her depression. In addition to taking the Zoloft, I asked Kate to monitor her symptoms daily by recording them on a log I provided. The log asks clients to record the severity of her symptoms on a scale of 1-10, with 1 being low and 10 being high.

The first week, she rated her symptoms at either 9 or 10. By the end of the fifth week, they had decreased to a range of two to five. Kate was happy with her progress and motivated to continue in therapy. In addition to her daily log, I asked her to begin exercising at least three times a week and to spend some time (at least one hour a week) writing poetry, painting, or doing some other enjoyable activity. My reasons for asking Kate to engage in these activities were two-fold: 1) help her to establish an identity that she could feel happy about, and 2) help her to improve her feelings of self worth.

During these weeks, I continued focusing on engagement, wanting to build a relationship that Kate had confidence in and trusted me as her therapist. I did this by monitoring my reactions to her, listening attentively, affirming her, and allowing her to set the tone and pace of our sessions. For instance, she came in one week feeling angry over a small incident at work. We spent the whole session on that. Another week she felt hurt by a comment her mother had made and we spent the session discussing this and other factors related to her relationship with her mother.

In solidifying a therapeutic relationship, I believe it is important for clients to feel they are in control of sessions as much as the therapist is. This does not mean that clients should completely trivialize sessions by talking about incidental details and non-pertinent information; it does mean that I am there to hear and integrate into the whole "assessment picture" what is relevant to clients at any point in time during our work together.

During our fifth session, I asked Kate if she would be willing to attend a support group for young mothers. She was reluctant, saying she did not think she could take the time to go to weekly meetings other than ours. I asked her to give it some consideration, but did not press the issue. She returned the following week, saying she did not care to attend the group because she did not have time. However, she did say that she felt better about herself as a mother.

As a social work practitioner, I must be careful to follow the NASW (National Association of Social Workers) Code of Ethics, which includes giving all clients the right of self determination. To me, this means that I allow clients to make choices according to their own values, needs, and judgments, regardless is it is what I would choose or want for my clients.

I asked Kate if she was ready to begin working on our second goal, to increase her marital satisfaction. She said that she was, indeed ready to begin that work. We discussed whether to ask Jason to join us and she said she would like to "get my thoughts together" first. I asked her what she meant by this comment. Kate stated that she wanted to explore what the marriage meant to her, to know what she was able to give, and where she had to "draw the line" before Jason met with us.

This was our sixth session, and we had originally talked about therapy lasting three months. I told were we were on target with our first goal and I had no reason to think we could not have a satisfactory resolution to the second goal in six more weeks. However, I assured her that we could take more time if necessary and that once Jason began coming and we negotiated goals for them as a couple. I said that I would make a determination of the length of time I projected to meet their goals. For the rest of the session, Kate told me about her ideas of what marriage should and should not be, and how her marriage fell short of the ideal marriage that she wanted.

Discovering Kate's Secrets

At our next session, Kate appeared anxious (repeatedly rubbed her hands together, which I had never seen her do) and tearful. I asked her if something had happened during the week. She told me that Jason had moved out after a big "blow up" about sex. When I asked her if she felt like talking about it, Kate began crying so hard she was trembling. After about five minutes, she collected herself and said, "I can't do this—I hope he doesn't come back."

We sat silently for a few seconds. Kate then explained that sometimes Jason was more understanding than other times. She said that sometimes she has no interest in sex, and other times she enjoyed it. I asked what was different about those times, using the solution-focused therapy technique of asking for exceptions. Kate stated that she did not know. I asked her how often she enjoyed having sex with Jason and how often she had no desire for it. She said that about two times out of ten, she enjoys it. However, sometimes even when she enjoys it, she might suddenly react negatively to a certain feeling or touch from Jason.

After our first session, I had wondered if her brother had physically, verbally, or sexually assaulted Kate. However, I was careful to hold this suspicion in the back of my mind and not confront Kate about it. When I had asked her about her childhood, Kate had simply told me that it was "ordinary." I had also wondered if her depression was rooted in her victimization in some way. Her maladaptive coping mechanisms she described further fueled my suspicions.

Bringing my thoughts back to the session, I referred to her description about reacting, at times, to certain feelings or touches and asked her why she thought that might happen to her. She began to cry, holding her face in her hands and at times shaking her head. I gently told her she could tell me whatever was on her mind. Kate slowly revealed, in a matter-of-fact way, that her brother, Tom, had sexually molested her repeatedly when she was young. I asked her age at the time. Kate said that the molestation began when she was seven or eight years old and stopped when she was 13.

Kate said that she had not told anyone except Casey, her girlfriend, and her grandmother. This was, of course, a huge revelation for Kate. I wanted to respect her need to divulge only as much information as she could handle, and at a pace she could handle. Rather than ask more questions, I shifted focus to a less intense level. To honor her survival skills and remind her of her strengths, I told her how strong she was to carry that "burden" all these years, and suggested that she must have felt alone. I told her she missed having a normal childhood and that it must have been hard to have a secret like that all her life.

Kate seemed relieved not to have to talk about it anymore, but had difficulty seeing her as having been successful at surviving. She said, "But I'm still a mess." I asked her if she had ever confronted Tom and she said no. He had moved across country when he was 18, just after the abuse ended. She had seen him on only twice since then. She stated that both times were awkward, with small talk, no affection, and no desire to spend any more time together than unavoidable. Our session ended that day with Kate saying, "I'm glad to finally talk about it."

Ethical Issues and Decision-making

At our team meeting (where we, as clinicians discuss cases) a few days later, I described my reaction to that session as emotionally and physically draining. That was the strongest reaction I had ever had to a session. However, in talking with my colleagues about it, we concluded that the intensity of a session such as that often has that effect on the clinician. It helped me to present the case and elicit valuable insights and suggestions from well-trained and respected people. Several of them talked about the need to debrief about cases and to make self-care a priority.

One colleague said that in order to continue to be effective as a therapist and avoid burnout, it is imperative to know our boundaries and to take care of ourselves, including our physical, emotional, intellectual, and spiritual needs. I wondered if I would have felt less reaction if I paid more attention to my own needs recently. I had been working longer hours, not taking time for exercise or adequate sleep, and had neglected some of my friendships because of time constraints.

I also had found it difficult, during some sessions with Kate, to remain intensely focused. I attributed this to my fatigue. After spending some time discussing this with my supervisor and clinical team, I determined, to make self-care a higher priority. I knew that this was my ethical and professional responsibility. Thai is, I cannot provide the best quality of care for my clients if I fail to be at my optimal performance level.

Setback in Kate's Treatment

Kate called to cancel her next appointment, leaving a message with the receptionist that she would call back to reschedule. I thought, "Oh no, she's bailing out of therapy because it became too intense for her, and she won't be back." Two weeks went by and I was surprised to get a call from Kate's mother saying that she was hospitalized for a suicide attempt (she had overdosed on medication).

Upon Kate's release from the hospital three weeks later, she came for an appointment with me. She said Jason had moved back home and that she wanted to work things out. We negotiated new goals, including:

Goals:
1. Monitor depressive symptoms
2. Confront issues related to past abuse
3. Adopt coping strategies to manage her roles and responsibilities

We agreed that we would meet weekly for three months and continue at weekly or biweekly meetings for another three months to achieve these goals.

Kate's progress during the first two months was slow. She was paralyzed with fear, anxiety, and emotional pain while attempting to confront the feelings she had carried since childhood like a weight around her ankles. Her survival mechanisms of avoiding the pain by abusing drugs and alcohol were no longer viable options. She did not want to expose herself to the reality of what had happened to her. Instead, she wanted to minimize what had happened and rationalize that she did not feel victimized. In this way, Kate "protected" herself from facing the trauma she had experienced and accepts it for what it was.

This type of denial demonstrated by Kate serves people experiencing trauma by allowing them to believe they are not experiencing the event(s). This denial is exhibited on a continuum from depersonalization, feeling outside oneself, to the development of multiple personalities. One of the ways Kate had dealt with her intense guilt and shame was to paint graphic pictures depicting anger and violence. She locked all of the paintings away in her chest. Only her friend Casey had seen them.

In the third month, Kate began gradually breaking through her denial. She became willing to talk more about her secret and how she managed to handle it over the years. She also talked about trying to give her mother clues about what happened on several occasions. However, her mother never got the hints. Her brother had threatened to kill her if she told anyone, and she believed him. Kate had only told her grandmother after the abuse had stopped, and made her promise not to break her confidence.

When we began addressing the impact of Kate's abuse on her current functioning, she decided she should share her "secret" with Jason and with her parents. Jason was accepting and supportive and this was of course, very helpful and reassuring to Kate. Her father was shocked, but supportive and caring. Kate's mother had the most difficulty believing and accepting what had happened. This was hard for Kate because she desperately wanted her mother to acknowledge her pain.

Since that time, Jason has come to two sessions with her to discuss the impact of what happened on their relationship. Both sessions were helpful to both of them. Kate's mother also attended a session to try to handle the reality of the news.

Kate's feelings of self blame, guilt, and shame were overwhelming at times. They had been an integral part of who she was over the years. Having to confront and displace these feelings was frightening. We spent time each week talking about how these past realities needed to be accepted in a different way now, through a shift in perspective. She needed to begin seeing herself as survivor rather than victim.

Since Kate's early childhood memories were happy ones, we spent time looking back at the years before the abuse began. We spent a lot of time talking about how her concept of self, trust, love, and acceptance were influenced by the abuse. Grieving the loss of innocence and what her missed childhood were hard for Kate. It was important, I felt, not to push her, but let her work through this pain in the time that she needed. We were into our fifth month when we extended our time-frame for another three months beyond the previously agreed on six.

Interventions

I used a number of different modalities and interventions throughout my work with Kate, drawing on what seemed most appropriate for the goals and objectives at a given time. Medication was essential to stabilize Kate's mood, but I firmly believe it was the combination of Zoloft and psychotherapy that resulted in a successful outcome.

I used behavioral interventions to help Kate cope with her depression and low self esteem she experienced. These included asking her to exercise, paint, and write poetry or do other enjoyable activities. When we began working on her issues related to the abuse, I asked her to journal regularly. This helped her to express her feelings and thoughts between our sessions in a healthy way. She also related her feelings in her poems and paintings and at times, brought in selected ones to share with me.

I implemented cognitive therapy techniques to help Kate identify and change negative self-talk and beliefs. I asked her to record what she thought or believed, or told herself, on a daily basis on a log I provided. I also asked her to explore the basis for these thoughts or beliefs and then to write a revised, more realistic belief. I asked her to bring in the log weekly to discuss the items on it. This was valuable for her and helped her adopt a more realistic image of herself and to improve her self esteem. It also helped her accept the fact that her abuse was not her fault and that self-blame was unjustified.

I used bibliotherapy with Kate. I asked her to read *Secret Survivors* by Sue Blume. This book is about surviving incest. We discussed what Kate had read each week and this was very helpful to her. It was helpful because it included useful and practical survival techniques and because she realized that she was not alone in her feelings.

The use of solution focused techniques were useful, especially finding exceptions to certain problematic times. I asked Kate to scale her feelings about her improvements in mood, self esteem, and coping methods.

Gradually, over the next few months, Kate's depression lessened significantly. She integrated self blame, denial, guilt, and shame into her life in a way in which she could accept them as part of her past but did not depend on poor coping methods to handle them. Her relationship with Jason improved, and they spent several sessions together in working on their relationship. Kate's self esteem had healed and she could see her strengths, as a survivor. She also began to think of herself as a valuable person, as a wife, mother, painter, poet, and even daughter.

Termination

Kate and I had often talked about having some significant event to mark her successful conclusion to the treatment process. We had talked about the possibility of her confronting Tom about the incest and this being a successful outcome to her therapy. However, as progress continued, her desire to confront Tom diminished. She did not feel it was necessary, or even desirable, as an outcome. We measured success by the progress she had made in meeting our goals. She decided to write a poem about her success and her ability to think of herself as a survivor rather than a victim. In our last session, she brought this poem and shared it with me.

I asked her to call me in three months to let me know how things were going. She did, and happily reported that she and Jason had bought a small place of their own and recently moved. She said this had helped their relationship, and that Tim still spends time with her parents during the week.

Evaluation of Practice

I evaluated Kate's treatment by looking at whether or not she met her treatment goals. Although there were setbacks in the progress of therapy, there were successful conclusions. Since this was also the basis for termination, I asked Kate about her satisfaction with the therapeutic process. She said that although it had not been easy, that she was pleased with the outcome and felt that she had, for the first time in her life, been able to see herself as a worthwhile person.

Questions _____

The author presented an interesting, successfully terminated case that involved many issues commonly found in practice with sexual abuse cases. Taking a broad view of this case, reevaluate the author's work and your participation through the questions asked throughout the case.

1. Review Kate's progress in treatment. Based on the author's description, the professional literature, and the latest practice evidence, what occurred to account for her progress?
2. What was the theoretical approach or combination of approaches that appeared to work best for Kate?
3. What additional intervention(s) would you recommend? Use the professional literature and latest practice evidence to justify your recommendations.
4. Overall, what is your professional opinion of the work performed in this case? As always, refer to the professional literature, practice evidence, your experience, and the experience of peers when developing your opinion.
5. Based on your review, what additional or alternative approaches could the author have used with Kate? That is, if you were the practitioner, how would you have approached this case? Please explain and justify your approach.
6. What did the case demonstrate that you could use in other practice settings? List the most important issues you learned and their relevance in your future practice career.

3

Austin

Cathy Simmons

Austin is one of the few male clients in my career who came into therapy willing to reveal childhood sexual abuse in his first session. Now, I wish I could take credit for his readiness, but I cannot. I believe Austin came ready for treatment primarily because of his past as a client. That is, I was Austin's fourth therapist in recent years and I believe these experiences "prepared" him for our therapeutic relationship. Austin began his therapeutic journey several years earlier. Unfortunately, each therapeutic encounter followed the same path. After a short time in therapy, Austin "quit" each of his three previous therapists because they "pushed" him to discuss his childhood demons. Thus, each therapist deemed him a treatment "failure."

It is unfortunate that many practitioners see unfinished treatment as failures. Some practitioners blame themselves for the failures, but I have seen many more practitioners blame their clients, restating the mantra, "They were unmotivated," or, "They were resistant." In my opinion and experience, defining unfinished treatment attempts as failures is often shortsighted. As Austin's case demonstrates, sometimes an unfinished treatment attempt actually prepares clients for future engagement and treatment success. For Austin, his past unfinished treatment attempts and a strong relationship with his wife laid the foundation for his ultimate success. So, instead of taking all of the credit, it became clear that Austin arrived in my office "ready to work."

At no time during Austin's previous three treatment attempts did he directly address his childhood sexual abuse. Instead, these therapies addressed several symptoms of his underlying problem: teenage acting out, anger management, and substance abuse. The "red flags" that previously brought him into therapy led practitioners to question Austin about possible childhood sexual abuse. However, as with many sexual abuse survivors, Austin was not ready to deal with his victimization, so he did not (Davis & Bass, 1994; Hunter, 1900: Lew, 2004). Austin presented in my office with multiple problems typical of sexual abuse survivors including failed treatment attempts, a history of self-medication, questions about his sexuality, issues of trust, and a fear of fatherhood.

Questions

Before moving on with this case, reflect on the author's comments about treatment "failures." The author claimed that many more practitioners blame clients for drop-out (failure) than they blame the treatment or approach. Usually seeing client drop-out as a sign of a lack of motivation to change, many practitioners choose to blame clients without critically examining their own contribution to the lack of engagement. Indeed, clients may not drop-out because they do not want to change, but are afraid to move forward. Given all the possibilities involved in this common phenomenon, please respond to the following questions.

1. **Examine the professional literature regarding client drop-out and/or unsuccessful treatment and the factors involved in such. What does the literature have to say about this issue, especially pertaining to cases of sexual abuse?**

2. **Discuss with peers or colleagues their experience with client drop-out as practitioners or, perhaps when and if you or your peers/colleagues ever dropped-out of therapy in their own personal lives. What are/were the reasons for this happening?**

3. **Critically examine what you have learned from teachers and other professionals about client drop-out in the context of your personal beliefs about this issue. What are the implicit and explicit messages being communicated about clients who drop-out of care? Do these same people view clients differently depending on presenting problem or treatment setting (i.e., mental health problems versus sexual abuse, etc.)?**

Client Engagement

Intake Assessment

Austin arrived at his 90-min, new client intake assessment with his wife. While they arrived together, Austin wanted to meet alone at first. After the normal review about the limits of confidentiality and other needed administrative formalities, I asked him why he chose to make an appointment at the clinic for therapy. Austin began his story matter-of-factly, by saying, "John, my mother's old boyfriend, use to make me have sex with him."

His straightforward and matter-of-fact approach surprised me. I have never had a male sexual abuse survivor begin the first minute of the first session in so forthcoming a manner. Usually, male sexual abuse survivors hide their abuse by presenting a slew of other problems ranging from addiction, to depression, to self-mutilation—in fact, almost anything but sexual abuse (Davis & Bass, 1994; Hunter, 1900: Lew, 2004). The sexual abuse often comes out later in therapy, after trust is established and I have created a safe environment. Austin presented differently, apparently ready to confront his childhood demons.

Previous Therapy

Austin was no stranger to therapy. A year after John left the family; Austin's mother took him to a social worker to address his "acting out" behavior at home and school. He described this experience as "a joke" because he told the therapist and his mom "what they wanted to hear," then went out and did "whatever I wanted to do anyway." In describing his first therapeutic experience, Austin expressed significant anger at his mother for not protecting him and at the therapist for not knowing what happened. After four meetings with this therapist, he talked his mother into leaving him alone and letting him stop the sessions. Although Austin described this experience with distain, he also discussed some important things he learned from the experience. First, he got the idea that his mother really cared about him and tried to do what was best for him. He also began to get the idea that acting out did not work for him.

Although he learned little about himself from his first attempt at therapy, Austin still grappled with the remnants of his sexual abuse. He struggled with shame and denial manifesting itself as anger and addiction through his teenage years and his early twenties.

On two separate occasions, he attended substance abuse assessment appointments. The first time was the year after graduating from high school. Following a three-day "drunk" where he "doesn't remember" everything that happened, he attended a "few" Alcohol Anonymous (AA) meetings and an intake assessment at a community addictions program. At the time, they diagnosed him with alcohol abuse and recommended a treatment program that included 90 AA meetings in 90 days as well as total abstinence. Disagreeing that he had a problem, he did not "go back there," continuing to party and "goof around" for a few more years.

Austin's third treatment attempt occurred when he was 22 years old. Many of the people he knew in high school were graduating from college and getting good paying jobs. Austin was working in a record store making minimum wage. Sometimes his partying was "out of control," while other times he avoided "the scene altogether." He liked getting high because it numbed his feelings. However, he also liked the feeling of control he had when he was not drinking or smoking marijuana.

After a brief period of partying with some of his workmates who were graduating from college, he began questioning his lifestyle. A co-worker recently discharged from an addictions program encouraged him to attend a substance abuse assessment appointment. Austin's mother agreed to pay for it, grateful that her son was reaching out for help.

At about the same time, he enrolled in an EMT training program at the local community college. In this program, he began having success that he had not experienced before. His partying decreased as his success increased. After getting his first job, Austin decided that "partying" was not as good at numbing the pain as being successful at work. Hence, he stopped drinking and partying altogether, throwing himself into his work. Long hours at work and school allowed Austin to compartmentalize his life and avoid the pain from childhood.

During our appointment, Austin discussed his three previous attempts at therapy with thoughtful regard. He stated that each therapist in the past regarded him as a "treatment failure." Yet, Austin said that he learned a lot about himself nonetheless. With each attempt, he grew stronger. While he did not succeed according to therapist-imposed treatment goals, Austin learned enough to begin changing his life in positive ways.

When I train new social workers, I call this the "mayonnaise jar theory" to reframe difficult work that may seem unproductive into positive movement toward client change. Although many textbooks do not address this, practitioners in the field need to understand it. The "mayonnaise jar theory" simply points out that often, when opening a mayonnaise jar, the first few attempts to get the lid off often does not finish the job. One tries, but often needs different ways and methods to remove the lid. For example, running the jar under cold water, breaking the glue with a knife, and/or using a special jar-opening device might help. Although the lid does not come off right away—on your timetable—over time the lid does manage to loosen and finally come off. Changing methods or persons to remove the lid does not mean that the original methods did not work. The original work probably made the lid come off easier for the next person or the next method.

Success and failure—especially in therapy—comes in degrees, not absolutes. Instead, what matters is small movement toward change on client's time schedules. Hence, the incremental work of his three previous therapists probably helped prepared Austin for our relationship. For this reason, I reframed his past attempts at therapy in a positive light, focusing on his strengths, not his past failures.

Client Assessment Information

Background Information–Work and School

Austin is a 30-year-old Caucasian male working as an Emergency Medical Technician (EMT) in a medium size town located in western United States. He is 5'8" with a slender build, brown eyes, and short blond hair. Usually, Austin presents clean-shaven and neatly dressed in jeans, collared shirts, and cowboy boots. However, during particularly difficult weeks at work, he appeared tired and worn with sunken eyes and disheveled and sometimes dirty clothing.

For the past eight years, Austin's life revolved around his work. It had always been easy to throw himself into his job by pulling extra shifts and working late hours. Sometimes his days were hectic in a "crazy sort of way," not allowing him a chance to take a break. However, Austin liked it that way. When he worked, he felt good about himself. He felt like a modern day cowboy saving people's lives and making the world a little better without having to get to know anyone. This was the perfect arrangement for Austin because he did not trust people easily.

In his free time, Austin took biology and physical science classes at a local university. Although he hated school as a teenager, he loved it as an adult. After receiving "barely passing" grades in high school, Austin finished his high school diploma "by the skin of my teeth." For the next five years, he "messed around" working a number of menial jobs, partying, drinking, and smoking pot. During that time in his life, Austin's mother talked him into attending a substance abuse assessment. Although he hated the experience—swearing to "never talk to another social worker again"—it helped Austin realize that his lifestyle was getting him nowhere in life.

Through serendipity, he landed in an EMT training program at the age of 23. Despite not completing substance abuse treatment, Austin completed EMT certification "clean and mostly sober." Liking the success he felt in the EMT training program, Austin continued taking classes at the local community college. He eventually earned an associates degree in physical science "one class at a time." When we met, Austin was working on his bachelors' degree, maintaining a 4.0 GPA and planning to attend medical school following graduation.

Family of Origin and Sexual Abuse

Describing his childhood as "crazy," Austin was an only child raised by a single mother in a medium size town less than 100 miles from his current hometown in the southwest. With minimal support from her family, Austin's young mother was often out of work and changed residences frequently. Her personal life included a stream of relationships lasting from as short as few weeks to as long as four years. She wanted each of her "boyfriends" to become Austin's next father. Hence, Austin became used to a "parade" of new "fathers" in his life. Yet, since they never stayed around long, he did not have to get to know or trust any of them.

John was different. John became the only man in his mother's life that took a serious interest in him. Some of mother's boyfriends were kind to Austin, some ignored him, and some were mean. John jumped right into the family and took Austin under his wing. In fact, when asked to discuss significant male figures in his life, the only man he mentioned was John, his mother's boyfriend of four years.

John and his mother lived together for four years beginning when Austin was seven years old. Before that time, Austin remembers having a relatively happy childhood, receiving "average" grades, and liking his teachers. When John arrived, everything in Austin's life changed. At first, the changes were for the better. John was a handsome man who treated Austin and his mother well—"better than anyone had before," Austin claimed. His mother loved the idea that Austin finally had a "father," and did everything she could to encourage the relationship. She arranged their lives so Austin and John to spend a lot of time alone together and "father and son."

To Austin's mother—and Austin at first—John's presence in their lives was a "dream come true." John took Austin horseback riding, played ball and did other things fathers and sons do together. They ate dinner together. They spent genuine quality time together as "father and son," and as a family. All was finally going well in Austin and his mother's life.

Yet, all was not well in paradise. Shortly after his mother and John met, John began sexually abusing Austin. The abuse included fondling, oral sex, and anal penetration. It seemed that every time Austin and John were alone together, their time included sexual abusive contact. According to Austin, John's sexual abuse lasted the entire four years of their relationship.

Nobody ever discovered the "secret." Austin kept the abuse secret under a veil of threats against himself and his mother. Besides, he did not believe anyone would believe him anyways. Moreover, he did not want to ruin the first long-term significant relationship his mother had for years. He was afraid that his mother would not love him if he revealed his secret and John had to leave. Additionally, Austin was not entirely sure his mother would believe him.

As Austin grew older, John lost interest in him and the family. Apparently, John only "liked" younger boys and not adolescents. After four years of abuse, John left Austin's mother to move in with another woman who had an elementary school aged son.

As the years passed, Austin could not bring himself to reveal his childhood sexual abuse to anyone, especially therapists who were strangers to him. Therefore, John kept his secrets and did his best to cope with life as an untreated sexual abuse victim. As stated earlier, even during his first attempts at therapy, Austin was not ready to share his childhood sexual abuse experiences. Because they were strangers, Austin distrusted therapists because, as he said to me, they "pushed" him and told him things he "didn't want to hear."

Similar to most childhood sexual abuse victims, John felt that any revelation of the abuse betrayed his mother and John. When they were together, Austin said he genuinely loved John. John was the closest thing to a father Austin ever had, and he believed that he should be thankful to John for being there for his family.

Although Austin was happy that the abuse ended, he continued struggling with self-blame and guilt over John's leaving. Instead of focusing on the end of the abuse, Austin only seems to remember how sad his mother was when John left. Through the course of our discussion about John's leaving, Austin talked about feeling guilty for not "being good enough" for John to stay. This guilt, mixed with feelings of relief that the abuse was over, created significant pain and stress for Austin as he moved through daily life. In many ways, Austin felt sad that his family dissolved when it did. Feelings of guilt, self-blame, and remorse intertwined with feelings of anger, fear, and shame is common for male sexual abuse survivors (Hunter, 1990: Lew, 2004). This "picture" describes the Austin I met perfectly.

Family of Creation

On the day of our first session together, Austin's marriage to Sally had lasted six months and his wife was pregnant with their first child. Sally was a laboratory technician in one of the hospitals Austin's EMT company serviced. She also took classes at the local university hoping to become an RN, "someday." They met at school and took a "long time" to become friends, even longer to start a romantic relationship.

However, it did not take long for Sally to become pregnant once they began dating. Once she became pregnant, Austin wanted to "do the right thing" so he agreed to marry her and begin a family. Because he never knew his father, Austin said that he felt compelled to be a good father. Additionally, he also wanted to be the kind of husband to Sally that his mother never had. By marrying his pregnant girlfriend, he could fulfill the manhood roles that he believed were missing in his own childhood. It was important for Austin to "be a good man." It never crossed his mind to do otherwise.

During our first session, Austin described his marriage to Sally as "happy," although he admitted to having trouble "opening up" to Sally. He portrayed himself as "emotionally distant." On one hand, Austin believed that men are supposed to be emotionally distant. However, on the other hand, Austin wanted to be different. He craved the ability to be an emotionally open and intimate partner with Sally, despite having no male role models in his life to serve as a guide in this way.

Austin said he struggled to trust his wife with his emotions, especially his history as a sexual abuse victim. His issues with Sally did not relate specifically to her as a person. She was a good person who deserved his trust. However, Austin said that he "cannot" trust anyone, even if people deserve his trust. According to Austin, Sally certainly deserved his trust, but he simply did not know how to proceed in the relationship.

Austin said that he struggled to express love for his wife. He simply could not bring himself to say that he loved her, to her face or otherwise. When asked about his feelings for Sally, Austin said he has "a great deal of respect" for her, calling her his "best friend," and "a wonderful person." When I asked him directly if he loved Sally, he smiled and said, "Yes, I do." Sexual abuse survivors commonly experience problems expressing feelings, trusting, and sharing aspects of self with others (Davis & Bass, 1994; Hunter, 1900: Lew, 2004). In his mind, Austin believed his childhood abuse secrets were "safe" as long as he did not become close to anyone. Now that he had Sally in his life, Austin said that he feared being unable to stay safe any longer because he would not be able to keep his feelings and experiences hidden forever.

Ironically, Sally was simultaneously a threat and a comfort to Austin. Not only was she his wife, someone Austin felt close to and loved, but she too was a sexual abuse survivor. Sally's stepfather sexually abused her for six years until she finally moved out of the house at 17 years old. She opened up to him early in their relationship. Hence, Austin felt even guiltier because of his unwillingness to share his abuse with Sally, made worse because she shared her abuse with him. Austin also said that he felt as if Sally "knew" already, simply by looking at him. He sensed that because she was a victim, she could "see it" in him. Obviously, her past and their relationship intimidated him.

Through the course of their friendship, dating, and early marriage, Sally began trying to help Austin begin speaking about his childhood sexual abuse. Austin said that he began slowly revealing aspects of his relationship with his mother and, ultimately John, with her. However, he said this was painful and he could not finish the story. Yet, according to Austin, Sally was the first person, before me, he ever told about John and the sexual abuse. However, he told me that he had not let Sally know the extent of John's abuse.

Additionally, Sally was also the one person (outside of Austin) most deeply affected by his abuse and the coping mechanisms he developed over the years. Austin said that he believed Sally tried helping him by sharing how her therapy helped her deal with her abuse history. Seeking therapy a few years before she married, Sally claimed that she found success in therapy dealing with her childhood victimization. The therapeutic process helped her reach the point where she could return to school and lead what Sally called a "semi-normal life." For this reason, Sally continued encouraging Austin to return to counseling and be honest about his history. Sally's support of the therapeutic process ultimately helped Austin come to therapy ready to be a successful client. They supported each other through their respective recoveries.

Client Presentation—Symptoms

Austin's world became progressively more difficult for him to control in the months leading up to our first session. Between getting married, opening up to his new wife, and pending fatherhood, Austin's safe world of secrets started unraveling. Ironically, despite his best efforts, Austin's world was organized in such a way that he had to face his past—or leave altogether. According to Austin, leaving was "not an option."

Austin reported that he always had trouble sleeping. His trouble included every aspect of sleep, including falling asleep, sleeping through the night, and vivid nightmares "every now and then." Recently, he reported that sleep became even more difficult. Shortly after his marriage—coinciding with his first steps into his past with Sally—Austin said he began having intense nightmares almost every night. By the time we met, Austin said that he was getting only one or two hours of sleep per night and was continually "exhausted."

He also said that he began having intrusive thoughts (flashbacks) about specific abuse incidents. Simultaneously, impending fatherhood began to affect his wellbeing. Austin said that in recent weeks he had begun fearing that he would be abusive with his own child. He read somewhere people that sexually abused children were "all" abuse victims. Hence, he assumed this meant that he would abuse his child whether he wanted to or not. This thought repulsed him and certainly helped keep him awake at night.

As often happens, the more Austin thought about the changes in his life coupled with opening up to his wife about his childhood victimization, the more intensive his daily symptoms became. Austin began having trouble controlling his emotions, something he always prided himself on. He reported lashing out in anger at work and home and having trouble concentrating. Although he said that he "always" had to work to control himself and his anger before, as Sally approached her due date, he could not control himself as he used to when he was alone.

Questions _____

In the preceding discussion, Austin talked about being afraid of fatherhood, primarily because he feared that he might abuse his child. Over the years, many people—lay and professional—have interpreted the literature on sexual abuse in the same way that Austin did. That is, many laypeople and professional helpers believe that the literature says that "all" people who abuse children also were abused as children. Many extend that argument to believe that once abused, people automatically become abusers. This belief permeates the profession so

deeply that many States have developed public child welfare policy based on this "fact." Hence, before moving on with this case, please respond to the following issues either alone, in a small peer group, or in classroom discussion.

1. Go to the professional literature about sexual abuse. What, in fact, does the literature say about this issue? Please locate multiple sources and compare not only the findings, discussions, and conclusions, but also the research methods used to generate the findings, discussions, and conclusions. Before drawing your conclusions, is the research used to generate these ideas credible?
2. Now that you have developed a position based on multiple literature sources, look into the public policy arena in your State to determine what policies or rules of practice are based largely on the research. Specifically, do the policy initiatives in your State match the findings of credible research in the area?
3. Now formulate a discussion with peers about your findings and thoroughly discuss the implications of your research on practice. Perhaps, in a classroom setting you could design a debate to examine various aspects of this important issue in practice with sexual abuse victims and perpetrators.

Compartmentalizing

To keep his daily symptoms and memories at bay, Austin developed a lifelong strategy of hiding his feelings by staying busy and apart from significant others and trying to "forget" his past. Often referred to as compartmentalizing, the act of not letting feelings get in the way of productivity is a highly regarded trait in modern society (Bass & Davis, 1994; Lew, 2004).

So-called mentally healthy individuals integrate different aspects of their life into compartments, while remaining true to their basic feelings and inherent personality. For example, even though you have a hectic existence at work, you are able to put it aside when you go home and have a happy family life. In this way, compartmentalizing is a normal and healthy way for people to manage busy lives. However, most sexual abuse survivors have significant problems integrating various aspects of their lives in a way that allows them to carry on a normal, healthy life. That is, the boundaries between compartments either become solid and impenetrable (at an extreme this leads to dissociation) or so diffuse that people present as "out of control" (Bass & Davis, 1994; Lew, 2004).

Many sexual abuse survivors do not learn healthy ways of integrating their compartments in a way that allows them to feel in control of their lives (Bass & Davis, 1994; Lew, 2004). Often told by parents and perpetrators to "pretend" that nothing is wrong or to "forget" about the past, sexual abuse survivors usually become expert at keeping secrets. It is what they learn about life from role models and believe is normal and expected. To survive, abuse victims often learn to separate different aspects of their existence, putting their abuse into a rigid compartment separate from other parts of their lives. These people learn to live as if the abuse did not happen, and/or it does not matter if it did occur. To the sexual abuse survivor, it makes no difference if one's experience contradicts another experience. He (or she) simply works to keep each experience in separate compartments so that they do not interfere with each other.

For example, Austin reported feeling warmth and love for John while disliking the abuse and knowing it was wrong. Similar to Austin, the sexual abuse survivor may like the attention they receive from perpetrators, so they put the abuse into a compartment separate from the rest of their experience. For the sexual abuse survivor, rigid compartmentalizing is the only way to deal with conflicting information (Bass & Davis, 1994; Lew, 2004). This often "works" until the pressure of life breaks the rigid boundaries down, leading to people feeling and acting out of control.

The lives of sexual abuse survivors are often fragmented (Bass & Davis, 1994; Lew, 2004). Because survivors learn to compartmentalize their feelings and experiences secretively and cannot share their pain with friends, teachers, or other family members, their life often becomes simply about controlling their compartments. That is, control over information and interaction is paramount. The more personal information one shares, the harder it becomes to maintain compartment boundaries and/or the more likely one believes others will misuse and abuse the information. In other words, they fear their secrets will be revealed. For this reason, sexual abuse survivors tend to separate themselves or parts of themselves from others. That way, they are closed to surprises, violated trust, conflicting roles, or unwanted feelings. They keep their lives fragmented, sharing small pieces of themselves, but controlling the information and not sharing all of themselves with anyone (Bass & Davis, 1994; Lew, 2004).

Austin's Experience

Prior to his marriage, Austin found ways to keep his compartments separate. He spent most of the waking hours of his adult life in pursuit of work and school goals. Telling himself that real men were distant, Austin shared only small pieces of information with others, keeping his interpersonal relationships shallow and temporary. When he felt that he was getting too close to someone, he simply backed way by throwing himself into his work and school. It was a safe existence for him. He looked at himself as a cowboy, sometimes lonely and emotionally guarded, but always strong. Once he married and shared his past with Sally, Austin's fragmented life began integrating. Feelings he put away into secret compartments began spilling into the open for others to see. When Austin began feeling genuine feelings of love toward Sally and their unborn child, a whole range of emotions that he spent a lifetime repressing began triggering. Like dominos falling in a row, Austin's symptoms intensified.

Our Clinic

For the good of himself and his unborn child, Austin's wife talked him into attended a 90-minute intake appointment with me at our multi-disciplinary outpatient mental health clinic. The clinic provides both short and long term counseling to individuals and families with a variety of mental health and substance abuse related concerns. Sally also attended group therapy at the clinic for the past two years. During the intake assessment, Austin reported worsening symptoms of hyperviligiance, intrusive thoughts, irritability, and avoidance associated with memories of his childhood sexual abuse. Although the increasing severity of symptoms had only been present since his marriage and pending fatherhood, he reported varying levels of similar symptoms since childhood.

Questions

Now that the author has presented basic first session information about Austin's life, and before reading on in this case, please perform the following exercises based on your education, experience, the professional literature, and the available best practice evidence. To increase your learning potential, you may want to do this in a small group with other students in your course.

1. Based on the information provided above, construct a three-generation genogram, and eco-map that represents Austin's personal, familial, and environmental circumstances. What further information do you need to complete this exercise? What patterns do these two important graphical assessment tools demonstrate?
2. Based on the same information, construct a list of Austin's issues and strengths, drawing from multi-systemic sources.
3. Write a two- to three-page narrative assessment that encompasses Austin's multi-systemic issues and strengths. Review Chapter 1 if necessary. This narrative should provide a comprehensive and multi-systemic explanation of his life as he prepares to undergo therapy with the author. Importantly, what information is missing? What strategies would you use to gain this information from Austin, given his unique history and personal style?
4. Try identifying a theoretical model or approach that you would use to guide your assessment. According to the literature, what other theoretical options are available and how would these options change the nature of your assessment?
5. Develop multi-axial DSM-IV-TR diagnoses for Austin. Provide a list of client symptoms that you used to justify you diagnostic decisions. What, if any, information was missing that would make this easier?
6. Based on your assessment and diagnoses, develop a treatment plan for Austin that encompasses the information contained in your multi-systemic assessment. Be sure to include comments on the theoretical model and method(s) you would use were you Austin's therapist.

Strength's Perspective

The strength perspective is a valuable way to approach clients, beginning in the intake session. The strength's perspective is "an orientation in social work and other professional practices that emphasizes the client's resources, capabilities, support systems and motivations to meet challenges and overcome adversity" (Barker, 1999, p. 468). In practice, employing the strength perspective does not preclude discussing client problems (Barker, 1999). Instead, it emphasizes client assets in the process of achieving and maintaining their individual well-being.

Using a strength's based approach starts with a biopsychosocial assessment that includes spirituality, family of origin, family of creation, medical concerns, mental health history, childhood and adult abuse history, substance use, current symptoms, duration of problems, coping skills, and social supports.

This meant helping Austin link his assets and strengths to how he dealt with his childhood sexual abuse. Austin's assets included a supportive wife and work environment, financial security, personal organization, multiple personal achievements, and a spoken desire to begin changing in order to be a good husband and father. Utilizing these strengths, I started helping Austin to educate himself about the experience of being a survivor of childhood sexual abuse and then moved on to tap into his motivation for therapy.

Education as Part of the Intake Process

I began tapping into Austin's drive to learn—an identified strength—during the intake assessment. I provided him educational materials to reinforce concepts introduced during the session and provide alternative explanations for issues most affecting him. Providing reading material about childhood sexual abuse and PTSD, helped Austin engage in a more detailed discussion about his experiences, problems, and coping mechanisms (e.g. compartmentalizing, avoiding, commitment to work, alcohol and other drug use, etc.)

Our discussion then moved to ideas about how specific aspects of his life did not work for him any longer (e.g., keeping secrets was negatively affecting his marriage). From understanding why he did what he did, Austin and I began generating ideas for treatment and intervention planning. Focusing on the things Austin did well, including aspects of his career, education, and positive aspects of his marriage were all part of the strengths approach. Focusing on Austin's strengths helps him verbalize the changes he wanted to make in his life without feeling hopeless about himself and his problems.

Austin's Diagnosis: Posttraumatic Stress Disorder

The intense symptoms Austin described during our first meeting were consistent with Posttraumatic Stress Disorder or PTSD (American Psychiatric Association, 2000). PTSD is an anxiety disorder that occurs when a person is exposed to an event or series of events where they, "experienced, witnessed, or was (were) confronted with an event or events that involve actual or threatened death or serious injury, or a threat to the physical integrity of self or others" and their "response involved intense fear, helplessness, or horror" (APA, p. 467). Referred to as traumatic events, these experiences may include accidents, natural disasters, manmade disasters, military combat, war, motor vehicle accidents, violent crime, rape, sexual assault, and/or any other unusual event that humans sometimes experience. For Austin, the traumatic event(s) included his four-year experience as a child victim of sexual abuse.

In addition to exposure to traumatic events and feeling fearful, helpless, and/or horror during the event, three classifications of distressing symptoms must also be present at the time of diagnosis: (a) people must have occasions where the re-experience the trauma, also known as flashbacks, (b) experience periods of avoidance and emotional numbing, and (c) experience increased arousal (APA, 2000).

Clients often re-experience the trauma through nightmares, intrusive thoughts, acting or feeling as if the trauma were reoccurring, intense psychological distress, and/or physiological reactivity to cues that represent some aspect of the traumatic event. Avoidance and numbing often shows through the presence of symptoms such as avoiding reminders of the traumatic event at all cost, being unable to have loving feelings, memory loss, decreased interest in activities, and/or expecting to die early. Increased arousal includes difficulty sleeping, hypervigilance, exaggerated startle responses, difficulty concentrating, and/or irritability. For these symptoms to indicate a diagnosis of PTSD, at least one symptom related to re-experiencing the trauma, three symptoms of avoidance and numbing, and three symptoms of increased arousal must be present.

To make an accurate PTSD diagnosis, remember that the client's symptoms cannot occur randomly. Instead, client symptoms must somehow link to the traumatic event. That is, "intrusive images or thoughts are typically of some aspect of the actual event, not just random content that comes to mind in a distressing and intrusive quality and cannot easily be dispelled once it has entered consciousness" (Litz & Gray, 2001, p. 3). Additionally, to indicate a diagnosis of PTSD, client symptoms could not be present prior to the trauma and must persist for longer than one month following the traumatic event (APA, 2000). Although Austin's symptoms had been milder prior to his life changes, each was present in varying degrees since the abuse he experienced as a child. Hence, Austin's description of his life and his symptoms fit into the diagnostic criteria for PTSD (APA, 2000).

Additional Issues for Treatment

Austin's case generated three additional areas to consider when planning and conducting treatment. These issues are: (1) feelings of shame about his abuse, (2) sexuality confusion and homophobia, and (3) men and feelings. These three dimensions influence many aspects of practice with male sexual abuse survivors and play a significant role in Austin's treatment.

1. Shame. Many survivors of childhood sexual abuse struggle with issues of shame (Bass & Davis, 1994). Shame is the "painful feeling of having disgraced oneself or those one cares about because of an intentional act, involuntary behavior, or circumstance" (Barker, 1999, p. 440). Austin felt shameful on many levels. On one level, Austin believed he had the power to prevent his abuse. As a male and an only child with a single parent, Austin was the "man of the house" long before John arrived on the scene. Reporting to be "old for my age," he took charge of several household activities like the dishes and dinner making sure his mother was "taken care of." Because of his early independence, Austin felt he "should" have had more control over his abuse and "should have stopped it."

On another level, Austin felt shame for letting the abuse continue for so long. He remembered the good times with John, feeling that somehow he "caused it to happen" because he liked John and liked being a part of a family. His shame went deeper than simply feeling like he could have stopped it. Through introspective therapy, Austin discovered core beliefs that told him he "is a bad person" because he "let it happen so John would stay around." My hope was to help Austin replace his feelings of shame with a sense of empowerment. That is, I hoped he could reach the point where he believed that being a sexual abuse survivor did not necessarily mean being a lifelong victim. He was not to blame for his abuse and could not control or stop it. However, he could control of his recovery and whether or not he allowed the past to affect his life.

2. Sexual Confusion and Homophobia. A second area of concern related to Austin's stated sexual confusion and homophobic feelings. It is common for male survivors of childhood sexual abuse to struggle with issues of sexuality and homophobia (Hunter, 1990; Lew, 2004). Many male sexual abuse survivors report sexual performance anxiety and/or promiscuous behavior as attempts to prove their "manhood." Heterosexual male sexual abuse survivors often wonder whether they will ever have a "normal" sex life with women (Hunter, 1990; Lew, 2004). These fears often manifest in homophobic attitudes and behaviors (Lew, 2004).

During adolescence, Austin reported many behaviors indicative of sexual confusion, including promiscuity and homophobia. In therapy, Austin began early in the process discussing his concerns about being a good husband and father. Underlying his fears was a concern that his sexual abuse (and perhaps, his secret fear of being gay) made him "not man enough" to sexually satisfy his wife. Throughout early therapy, these issues frequently arose. My plan was to have Austin's independent work outside the therapeutic setting coupled with individual therapy to help him deal with his confusion, anger, and fear of being gay. In turn, the ultimate goal was to have Austin's fears about his sexual preference and performances diminish.

3. Men and Feelings. The third area of concern related to the normal difficulties that heterosexual men have regarding their emotions. Western culture tends to categorize men that compartmentalize their feelings as "strong," and men that express their feelings or talk about their problems as "weak" or effeminate (Lew, 2004). Western media routinely portrays images of males being emotionally restricted, independent, strong, fearless, independent, invulnerable, and in control. Popular culture portrays men as having difficulty expressing feelings and vulnerabilities while fearing intimate relationships and sometimes dependant. These images of maleness often conflict with the nature of the therapeutic process. That is, almost by definition those who enter therapy—either male or female—are vulnerable to some degree.

Since Austin learned his ideal of masculinity and maleness primarily from watching television and reading books, he internalized much of the western male ideal. Moreover, his primary male role model was John, a sexually abusing male that victimized Austin as a child. Hence, Austin struggled when discussing his feelings and admitting to victimization. He found it difficult to reconcile his victimization and intense emotions and his conception of the ideal male. Therefore, in therapy I intended to confront his ideas about what made a strong man in hopes of changing his image of strength. This may help Austin deal with his past and allow him to accept help in the present.

Questions

The author addressed three compelling issues to consider in treatment with Austin. Before moving on in the case, are there other compelling issues that you believe must be included in this discussion? If so, explain the issues and discuss the reasons you believe make them important to the case.

Treatment Plan

Our mental health clinic uses a managed care model. In this system, similar to many managed care models, clients must meet several criteria before receiving services. Among the criteria are, (1) preauthorization for services, (2) appropriate diagnosis for presenting symptoms, (3) having a treatment plan with congruent goals, and (4) progression toward those goals as determined through utilization review (Edinburg & Cottler, 1996). Because Austin met the DSM-IV-TR criteria for Posttraumatic Stress Disorder (APA, 2000), he was eligible for services through our managed care system. To ensure that clients understand their diagnosis, it is best to discuss with them their diagnosis and why they met the criteria before writing their treatment plan. With Austin, I discussed his treatment goals at the end of the first session and continued revising his goals after he indicated that he understood his diagnoses.

Because Austin's treatment plan included individual therapy and psycho-educational classes, it was appropriate to discuss his treatment plan at the conclusion of the intake assessment without writing it down in his clinical record. Instead, I offered Austin handouts to help develop goals for therapy. These handouts assist clients in deciding what they want to achieve in therapy. The handouts addressed ideas related to (a) what he felt was his primary problem, (b) his motivation for treatment, and (c) how life would change after successful treatment. Austin took the handouts home to think about them for the week between the intake session and his next appointment.

Although treatment planning starts with the first client contact, it is customary to write the formal treatment plan in session two or three (Granvold, 1994). Taking some time between the first two sessions gives clients time to process through the diagnostic information and think about their goals. The formal treatment plan is a contract between the client and practitioner. The practitioner agrees to provide services and the client agrees to participate in the activities indicated. Treatment plans should include (a) indicators of the type of activity, (b) frequency of each activity, (c) duration of treatment, and (d) who will be involved in each aspect of treatment. Additionally, providing clients with a copy of their treatment plan helps ensure that they understand their expectations. It also provides clients a greater sense of control over their problems while making them a partner in treatment (Gravold, 1994).

Treatment Options

I assessed Austin's symptoms as moderate during our initial meeting. Moreover, I did not sense that Austin held back or denied any underlying problems. His story appeared both honest and congruent. Most importantly, I assessed Austin as being highly motivated to change. For these reasons, I recommended individual therapy to help Austin work through issues related to childhood sexual abuse, PTSD, and change in life circumstances.

Additionally, because Austin experienced increased arousal and was re-experiencing his trauma at work and home, I recommended he see a psychiatrist to address potential medication management issues. However, because of his history with drugs and alcohol, Austin wanted to try managing his symptoms without medication. I believe clients must be free to choose their treatment path. Therefore, I decided not to push him into taking the psychiatric referral.

Instead, I used brief, cognitive-behavioral therapy techniques to help Austin control his immediate symptoms. Finally, to start the treatment process I employed a four-session psycho-educational class to provide basic information about mental health. Austin was interested in taking the class and individual therapy. Hence, our initial treatment plan included taking the class, starting individual therapy, and no medication to manage his symptoms.

Group Therapy

Group therapy has proven effective in treating survivors of childhood sexual abuse and incest (Higgins-Kessler, White, & Nelson, 2003). Often called survivors groups, the group process provides a supportive environment for individuals to deal with the symptoms of their abuse and develop healthy strategies for living (Bass & Davis, 1994; Hunter 1990; Lew, 2004.). Found in many United States communities, practitioners offer these groups in different formats. Some are highly structured, much like a traditional psycho-educational classes and focus on teaching different living skills to survivors. Others are free-flowing, such as a process-oriented group where the healing process of group therapy is lead by a professional practitioner. Still others are peer-support oriented, led by peer leaders in mutually beneficial non-therapeutic environments. Some groups are a combination of different methods. Whichever modality practitioners use, group work is an important component in treating survivors of sexual abuse and incest (Bass & Davis, 1994; Hunter, 1990; Lew, 2004)

In addition to a range of group types, different groups focus on different mixes of clients. Some groups consist of only female or only male survivors while some are open to both genders. In the community where Austin lived, the only survivor's group available was for women only. Primarily because of issues related to masculinity and sexuality, it is inappropriate to refer a male survivor of sexual abuse to a survivors group designed for and consisting of only women. For Austin, neither a male only group nor a mixed gender group was available. Therefore, we could not include group work in his treatment plan.

Questions _____

1. **Before moving on, compare the assessment and diagnostic statement you developed to the author's. Where do you find points of agreement and disagreement? Discuss these issues with peers and use the professional literature to analyze the differences.**

2. Compare the treatment plan you developed with the author's. Again, note any differences between your treatment plan and the author's.
3. What implications for treatment surfaced because of differences in assessment, diagnoses, and/or treatment planning?

Readiness to Change

As I stated earlier, Austin came into therapy ready to change in his life. His two primary concerns related to his marriage and impending fatherhood. He loved and trusted his wife and wanted to be a good husband. He also loved his unborn child and wanted to be a good father. Through life experience (previous therapy, professional experience, education, and his wife's childhood experiences) Austin knew that the only way he could become a good husband and father was to face his childhood sexual abuse.

Questions

Throughout this case, the author has discussed Austin's readiness for therapy, based on a number of life factors including three earlier attempts in therapy. The issue of assessing motivation is interesting and important for all practitioners. Therefore, before moving on in this case, consider the following:

1. Examine the professional literature on client engagement and motivation in therapy. Expand your search beyond sexual abuse cases, looking for the latest available literature on the subject. What models or ideas seem to represent best practice methods related to assessing motivation? How do these models or ideas apply to this case?
2. Related to sexual abuse, what does the professional literature say about male sexual abuse victims versus female victims? The author seems to imply that there are differences between male and female victims as clients, especially related to the engagement process. Are there any differences in treatment called for if the victim is male versus female in the literature? What does your experience and/or the experience of peers and instructors suggest about this topic?

Linking Theory to Treatment

A central task in the helping process involves practitioners linking practice issues to theories of helping. Practitioners cannot merely go into the practice setting with an idea that they will help clients without understanding how they are going to help. Theory tells practitioners how they are going to bring about change in the client's life and on what basis change will occur. Defined as "a group of related hypothetical concepts and constructs based on facts and observations that attempt to explain a particular phenomenon" (Barker, 1999, p.100), theory provides support for treatment activities. Theories also provide a plan that guides practitioners through client interactions. That is, theory provides the reason why practitioners do what they do with clients. Good practitioners understand that a solid theoretical foundation provides the building blocks for responsible social work practice (Turner, 1996).

Although theory provides the basis for practice, no single theory encompasses all clinical possibilities. That is, theory does not come in a one-size-fit-all format (Payne, 1997). "Theory is constantly changing in response to practice constructions ... accounts of its nature cannot be universal" (Payne, p. 24). When working with clients, social workers can use many different theoretical orientations. By integrating several theories, practitioners provide a broad helping process.

However, practitioners cannot insist on being true to any specific theory. Defined as using "a collection of certain aspects of various theories or practice methods that appear to be most useful for practice interventions" (Barker, 1999, p. 146), combining two or more therapeutic methods is often referred to as an eclectic approach. However, each activity in the eclectic approach needs to have a theoretical backing for its use.

In this case, Austin's strengths and needs drove how I incorporated an eclectic approach into his treatment regime. Primarily based on cognitive behavioral theories and insight-oriented approaches, the models of treatment I used with Austin included attending a psycho-educational class, participating in individual therapy, and doing independent work outside the treatment setting. By incorporating a variety of models and using techniques from a variety of orientations, I employed an eclectic approach to treatment that helped Austin deal with his presenting symptoms of PTSD, address his behavior patterns and fears while helping him process through his history of childhood sexual abuse.

Psycho-educational Class

At the beginning of treatment, Austin agreed to attend a four- session psycho-educational class that the clinic offered called, Introduction to Healthy Thinking. Focusing on basic ideas related to healthy lifestyles, this class addressed topics related to eating healthy, avoiding alcohol, and regular exercise, along with cognitive behavioral coping strategies including identifying thought distortions, disputing these distortions, and changing distorted thinking patterns.

Theoretically, the class used a cognitive behavioral approach, emphasizing how thoughts lead to feelings and actions. When clients can identify and change problematic thinking patterns, they can change the subsequent maladaptive feelings and behaviors. Over the course of four 90-minute sessions, clients learn, practice, and discuss how to replace distorted thought patterns with new thoughts that contribute to more desirable actions (Beck, 1967; Beck, 1988; Beck, Rush, Shaw & Every, 1979; Burns, 1999; Greenberger, & Padesky, 1995).

Austin reported feeling comfortable in class, participated appropriately, and completed the homework assignments. From his participation in the class, he began learning how much he could control his thoughts, moods, actions, and feelings. Many of the ideas covered in class Austin said he "kinda knew." Attending the class helped him better understand himself and gain a better sense of control over his presenting symptoms.

Individual Therapy

To address Austin's presenting PTSD related symptoms; I used a cognitive-behavioral approach that tended to be short-term, focused on the present, and addressed specific goals (Granvold, 1994). Cognitive behavioral therapies (CBT) are "approaches to treatment using selected concepts and techniques from behaviorism, social learning theory, action therapy, functional school of social work, task centered treatment and therapies based on cognitive models" (Barker, 1999, p. 84). CBT is an excellent tool to help clients reduce presenting symptoms (Granvold, 1994). Research also shows that CBT is effective in treating PTSD (NIMH, 2002). Consequently, the CBT approach was appropriate for Austin.

In addition to wanting to relieve his immediate PTSD related symptoms, Austin also wanted to explore his lifelong pattern of compartmentalizing and "pretending nothing is wrong." By voicing a desire to look deeper into his actions for greater insight, he was an excellent candidate for the evaluation of self, values, and feelings inherent in insight-oriented psychotherapy. Insight therapies are "treatment approaches oriented toward helping individuals achieve greater self-awareness and understanding of their conscious and unconscious motivations, emotions, thought processes, and underlying reasons for behavior" (Barker, 1999, p. 243). Although we decided to use CBT methods with Austin, we also used insight-oriented techniques at strategic points in therapy, making Austin's individual therapy experience eclectic.

The eclectic approach—a combination of CBT and insight-oriented treatments—was appropriate for Austin because he needed to address his underlying unconscious thoughts and memories as well as current problems of living and PTSD symptoms. Specifically, in the therapeutic relationship we decided to address (a) survival strategies, (b) denial, numbing, and compartmentalizing, (c) self-image, (d) fears of fatherhood (fears of becoming an abuser), (e) problems with intimacy and physical touch and (f) anger, fear, and disappointment. Dealing with these issues on the cognitive-behavioral level only, may not have been enough for him to deal with his childhood anger and the betrayal inherent with adult survivors of sexual abuse.

Questions _____

The author explained the treatment approaches she intended to use with Austin to help alleviate his symptoms and change his life. She provided a good rationale for her clinical decision-making in this case.

1. **Based on Austin's personal information, your experience, the practice literature, and best practice research and evaluation, critically analyze the author's decisions. What does the literature and best practice research say about the most effective treatment approaches for this case?**

2. **What approach or approaches would you employ if you were treating Austin instead of the author? Explain your rationale.**

Using the Strength's Perspective in Individual Therapy

When working with survivors of sexual abuse, practitioners must frame client's survival strategies and coping mechanisms positively (Bass & Davis, 1994; Lew, 2004) as part of the strength's perspective. Austin's survival strategies kept him alive through four years of sexual abuse, the aftermath in adolescence, and into adulthood. Early in individual therapy, I used a cognitive behavioral strategy targeted at helping Austin reframe his experiences into strengths.

As our relationship progressed, I used introspective techniques to help him understand how his unconscious coping mechanisms lead to developing intricate survival strategies. By helping him focus on how he succeeded with these strategies in the past, Austin realized that his old strategies no longer worked in his life. Once he understood how the connections between his past and his unconscious thoughts elicit current feelings and behaviors, he began making positive changes in his life, improving his self-image, and reducing his PTSD/anxiety related symptoms.

Addressing Austin's Specific Irrational Fear

Austin's main fear was that he would "become like John" once his child was born. That is, Austin feared that he would be compelled to sexually abuse his child because John sexually abused him as a child. In the cognitive/rational part of Austin's mind, he knew that he was not a sex abuse perpetrator. He neither found children sexually attractive nor felt powerless to the extent that he needed to exert sexual power over children. Austin also knew how his victimization injured his life. Hence, he verbalized that he "will never do that" to a child, his or anyone else's.

However, the fearful/irrational part of Austin's mind worried him. The research Austin did on sexual abuse survivors taught him that men who abuse children had been abused as children (Aylwin, Studer, & Reddon, 2003). Austin believed that there were significant differences between his abuser and himself. However, he recognized similarities as well. These perceived similarities triggered his irrational mind, leading to periods of overwhelming fear about his fitness as a future father. Through the course of therapy, Austin talked through his fears, discovered their origins and their irrationality. Once he understood his fears, he used self-talk and rationalization to dispute them when they resurfaced.

Independent Work

Independent work outside the therapeutic relationship is an important component in treating survivors of sexual abuse and incest. Independent work often comes in the form of self-education, journaling, and using art and music to describe and work thorough feelings. Through recommending books and informational handouts, practitioners can help clients educate themselves about sexual abuse and issues that survivors face. Additionally, the Internet is a good source for survivors for resources and connections with other survivors through topic-specific websites and/or chat groups.

Beyond self-education, journaling is an effective way for verbal and literate clients to process through their experience. Whether daily, weekly, or whenever they are experiencing a particularly difficult point in recovery, journaling can help clients verbalize feelings and organize problems. Finally, art and music are helpful tools for clients to use. Artistic expressions in the form of drawing, painting, sculpture, and/or music are methods even inarticulate clients and clients who have limited literate and cognitive abilities can use to process through experiences. By using self-education, journaling, and artistic expression, clients can independently process through their experiences.

Extremely motivated clients such as Austin generally find independent work rewarding. Starting with the handouts and a book I recommend, he began educating himself about the problem of sexual abuse and survivors' issues. By the time the therapeutic relationship ended, Austin was a nonprofessional expert on survivors' issues. Through learning strategies that other survivors used to thrive, Austin chose strategies appropriate for him. Austin decided that the most effective strategies were journaling and painting. Through daily journaling, Austin processed through the difficulties, fears, and joys of facing his past. Finally, Austin expressed some of his deepest feelings through painting.

Letter Writing

As an extension of the individual therapy process, I asked Austin to write letters to the various people in his life that had hurt him over the years. The first two letters went to John, for sexually abusing him, and his mother for not protecting him. He also wrote a letter to his father, a man Austin never met. Austin used letter writing to work through his feelings of anger, disappointment, frustration, and betrayal. Since Austin decided not to share his sexual abuse with anyone other than Sally and me, he did not send the letters. Instead, the purpose of writing the letters was to express his thoughts and feelings. Each letter became quite lengthy, going on for many pages.

Throughout his therapy, Austin frequently referred to the letters and their benefit to his treatment. He stated that writing honest letters allowed him to vent years of pent-up anger and provided him with significant emotional release. By the time we terminated treatment, Austin had a box full of letters stored in his closet. When things became especially difficult, he wrote another letter to deal with whatever bothered him. This process fit Austin's personal style. He found comfort in compartmentalizing parts of his life, putting the difficult memories away in the closet. He also alluded to possibly burning them someday. Austin still needs to hold on to his coping strategies that have been successful.

Ethical Issues and Decision Making

Austin's case presented several underlying ethical issues that affected my clinical decision-making process. "Ethical dilemmas occur in situations where the social worker must choose between two or more relevant, but contradictory, ethical directives, or when every alternative results in an undesirable outcome for one or more persons" (Loewenberg & Dolgoff, 1995, p. 8). In working with Austin, my ethical dilemma arose because of Austin's decision not to confront his abuser. The ethical issues of my client's desire to keep his abuse confidential and my duty to protect children from abuse contradict each other. By examining the underlying issues related to this ethical predicament, practitioners can think through how they would handle similar decisions in the future.

Austin's Decision to Not Confront/Report

Early in therapy, Austin informed me that he would not contact the authorities about his abuser. His unwillingness to contact authorities out of his need for confidentiality resulted in the potential for John to abuse other children. In fact, since a number of years had passed, it was likely that John had more victims since he left Austin's family. It was also likely there were other adult victims from the years before Austin. For practitioners, the NASW code of ethics (1999) outlines expectations regarding self-determination and confidentiality. However, state laws about reporting child abuse clearly indicate that whenever mandated reporters detect child abuse, they must report it to the appropriate authorities. In the case of an adult survivor revealing abuse from 18 years earlier, the law is not as clear. The conflicting values of self-determination and confidentiality for Austin and the potential for protecting children contradict each other and placed me in a difficult spot with Austin.

To add complexity to this ethical issue, Austin reported that he was "somewhat sure" that John was living with another family with young boys. Because Austin believed that John might be continuing to perpetrate, I weighed the balance between client confidentiality and a desire to protect potential victims. I consulted with the clinic's lawyer who advised me to report the incidents of child abuse to the proper authorities even though Austin provided minimal information about John and all of the information was hearsay. By keeping the informant confidential, I maintained Austin's confidentiality and alerted the proper authorities about a potential child abuser.

Questions

Eventually, every practitioner will confront the dilemma of deciding what to do around reporting real or suspected abuse to the proper authorities. The legal mandate for human service professionals to report abuse in a timely manner is central to the profession, codes of ethics, the legal system, and our communities. However, as the author stated, when the abuse occurred many years in the past and the issue becomes protection of future victims that might be abused, the law becomes unclear. Given the issues involved in this case, please consider the following issues.

   1. **Explore your state laws and policies regarding mandated reporting of abuse. What specifically do the laws and policies of your state require? What policies exist in your agencies and organizations regarding this issue?**
   2. **What does the law state regarding the specific issues involved in this case? Specifically, what is the duty to warn requirements on human service practitioners in your state? Does the duty to warn requirement apply in this case?**

3. Examine the code of professional ethics that applies to your profession. What does the code of ethics say about this particular dilemma?
4. Discuss this scenario with peers in small groups or as a class. If you were the practitioner, what decision would you make regarding Austin and his abuser? What additional issues must a responsible practitioner consider when making this decision?
5. What is your opinion of the author's choice? Did the author consider all the relevant issues before making this decision?

Termination

Termination begins during the intake session (Shulman, 1999). The sheer nature of the therapeutic relationship is temporary. Therefore, it is important for practitioners to help clients understand that their relationship with the therapist will end. From the beginning, Austin made it clear that he did not want to be in therapy "for the rest of his life." Keeping this in mind, we devised a treatment plan to help Austin understand that we started with a more intense plan and worked toward less frequent meetings as he improved.

When we began, Austin and I met weekly. After a few months, we moved to bi-monthly sessions. Eventually, we agreed to meet monthly. Nine months into our relationship, we decided to terminate treatment because Austin believed that he had improved. He reported that his PTSD symptoms were gone, his marriage was excellent, and his son was wonderful. He was about to graduate from college with his undergraduate degree and was preparing to apply to medical school. Although he enjoyed the therapy sessions, he understood that the therapeutic relationship was temporary (Shulman, 1999).

I planned the termination session one month prior to give Austin time to process the end of our relationship. During the final session, we discussed his progress, focused on his strengths, and planned how he would address symptoms if they resurfaced in the future. The final session ended with Austin understanding that he could always return to therapy if he felt the need.

Questions _____

The author presented an interesting, successfully terminated case that involved many issue commonly found in practice with sexual abuse cases. Taking a broad view of this case, reevaluate the author's work and your participation through the questions asked throughout the case.

1. Review Austin's progress in treatment. Based on the author's description, the professional literature, and the latest practice evidence, what occurred to account for Austin's progress?
2. What was the theoretical approach or combination of approaches that appeared to work best for Austin?
3. What additional intervention(s) would you recommend? Use the professional literature and latest practice evidence to justify your recommendations.

4. **Overall, what is your professional opinion of the work performed in this case? As always, refer to the professional literature, practice evidence, your experience, and the experience of peers when developing your opinion.**
5. **Based on your review, what additional or alternative approaches could the author have used with Austin? That is, if you were the practitioner, how would you have approached this case? Please explain and justify your approach.**
6. **What did the case demonstrate that you could use in other practice settings? List the most important issues you learned and their relevance in your future practice career.**

Bibliography

American Psychiatric Association. (2000). *Diagnostic and statistics manual of mental disorders* (4th ed.). Washington, DC: Author.

Aylwin, A. S., Studer, L. H., & Reddon, J. R. (2003). Abuse prevalence and victim gender among adult and adolescent child molesters. *International Journal of Law & Psychiatry, 26*(2), 179–190.

Barker, R. L. (1999). *The social work dictionary*. Washington, DC: NASW Press.

Beck, A. T. (1967). *Depression: Clinical, experimental and theoretical aspects*. New York: Hoeber. (Republished as *Depression: Causes and treatment*. Philadelphia: University of Pennsylvania Press, 1972.)

Beck, A. T., Rush, A. J., Shaw, B. F., & Emery, G. (1979). *Cognitive therapy of depression*. New York: Gilford Press.

Beck, A. T. (1988). *Love is never enough*. New York: Harper & Row.

Burns, D. D. (1999). *The feeling good handbook*. New York: Penguin Books.

Edinburg, G. M., & Cottler, J. M. (1996). Managed care. In Beebe, L., Winchester, N. A., Pflieger, F., & Lowman, S. (Eds.), *Encyclopedia of social work* (pp. 1635–1642). Washington, D C: NASW Press.

Gilligan, C. (1982). *In a different voice: Psychological theory and women's development*. Cambridge, Massachusetts: Harvard University Press.

Granvold, D. K. (1994). *Cognitive and behavioral treatment: Methods and applications*. Pacific Grove, California: Brooks/Cole Publishing Company.

Greenberger, D., & Padesky, C. A. (1995). *Mind over mood*. New York: Guilford Press.

Harrison, J. B., & Morris, L. A. (1996). Group therapy for adult male survivors of child sexual abuse. In M. P. Andronico (ed) *Men in groups: Insight, interventions, and psychoeducational work* (pp. 339–356). Washington, DC: American Psychological Association.

Higgins-Kessler, M. R., White, M. B., & Nelson, B. S. (2003). Group treatments for women sexually abused as children: A review of the literature and recommendations for future research, *Child Abuse & Neglect, 27*(9), 1045–1061.

Hunter, M. (1990). *Abused boys: The neglected victims of sexual abuse*. New York: Ballantine Publishing Group.

Lew, M. (1990). *Victims no longer: Men recovering from incest and other sexual child abuse*. New York, NY: Harper Collins Publishers.

Litz, B. T., Gray, M. J., & Bryant, R. A. (2002). Early intervention for trauma: Current status and future directions, *Clinical Psychology: Science and Practice, 9*(2), 112–134.

National Association of Social Workers (1999). *Code of ethics*. Washington, DC: Author.

National Institute of Mental Health (2002). *Mental health and mass violence: Evidence-based early psychological intervention for victims/survivors of mass violence. A workshop to reach consensus on best practices.* NIH Publication No. 02–5138, Washington, DC: U. S. Government Printing Office.

Payne, M. S. (1997). *Modern Social Work Theory, Second Edition*. Chicago, IL: Lyceum Books Inc.

Shulman, L. (1999). *The skills of helping individuals, families, groups, and communities* (4th ed.). Itasca, Illinois: F. E. Peacock Publishers, Inc.

Turner, F. J. (1996). Social Work Practice: Theoretical Base. In Beebe, L., Winchester, N. A., Pflieger, F., & Lowman, S. (Eds.), *Encyclopedia of Social Work* (pp. 2258–2265). Washington, DC: NASW Press.

4

Dani

Leslie Menhart

My first meeting with Dani occurred the day we admitted her to our long-term residential program for adolescents with mental health and delinquent behaviors. This initial meeting was memorable because Dani immediately said she hated me, followed by her calling me several inappropriate names I had not heard since high school. She quickly decompensated from there and began yelling at program staff that she would not follow the rules, they could not control her, and her mother would remove her from the program in a few days.

Within 10 minutes, Dani was sobbing and yelling threats. She ended on her hands and knees screaming obscenities at everybody in the room. Dani's behavioral display was dramatic. It appeared that she felt unsafe with her own behavior and in our program. Hence, I immediately designed a structure with rules and expectations for Dani to help her feel safer. Creating internal and external safety at the Macro and Micro levels became the foundation of her treatment over the next 24 months.

One of the unique aspects of this case was that several agencies worked together to help the entire family recover from the trauma of incest. For Dani and her family to succeed in treatment, I knew that I would have to work closely with other professionals working on the case, all of whom lived three hours away from the residential program where I worked and Dani now lived.

Multi-Systemic Assessment Information

Dani was a 13 year-old, bi-racial (Caucasian and Native American) female when I first met her in our residential facility. I was assigned as her therapist because she had a history of homicidal and sexually hurtful behaviors directed towards numerous younger children, including her younger male and female siblings. Because I had experience in these areas, we all felt that I was a good "fit" in terms of treatment needs of the client and treatment experience of the therapist.

I strongly suspected that Dani had been sexually abused, but she denied any abuse other than corporal punishment by her mother and step-father. I believed that the likely perpetrator of the sexual abuse was her deceased biological father. At the time Dani entered our program, she admitted to abusing seven younger children, including all her siblings.

Family History

Dani's parents married shortly after her birth. Her mother was Native American and father Caucasian. There was a 13-year age difference between them. Her mother had not grown up with traditional Native American customs, but did identify with some of her Native American culture and referred to herself as Native American. She indicated that Dani's maternal grandfather was of Native American and Scottish decent and her maternal grand mother was of German, Italian, and Hungarian decent. Dani's mother also indicated that Dani's father was Caucasian of European decent. Dani's father died when she was eight years old when another driver hit his car, killing him instantly. He was alone in the car when he died.

The marriage between Dani's parents was violent and controlling. Dani witnessed daily incidents of verbal abuse directed at her mother by her father. There were also weekly incidents of physical violence directed at Dani's mother by her father. Dani recalled many of these incidents. Dani's mother reported that Dani's father forced her to perform sexual acts against her will that were humiliating and/or physically painful. Although the father died several years before I met the family, mother continued to have deep fear of him and felt disgusted with herself for marrying him.

Dani's parents divorced when she was five years-old. Her father moved to a town approximately 90 miles away from where Dani and her mother lived. He became involved with various women and fathered additional children, one of whom died under questionable circumstances while in his care. Dani maintained visitation with him for two weekends per month and six weeks in the summer. She resided with her mother the remainder of the time.

Her mother became involved with various men, but did not have additional children until after she remarried when Dani was seven years old. Several of mother's male friends between marriages were verbally and/or physically abusive towards her. Dani said that she liked one or two of them, but would purposely behave in a disruptive and inappropriate manner towards them to ensure that they would not marry her mother. She indicated that she wanted her mother "all for herself." However, Dani did say that she "liked" her stepfather.

The Sexual Abuse Begins

Around the time Dani began visiting her father; mother noticed a significant change in Dani's behavior. Dani's mother reported that prior to Dani's visitation with father she was a typical five year-old kid in terms of behavior, social interactions, and cognitive development. Mother stated that after Dani's first visit with her father, she noticed immediate and significant negative changes in Dani. She indicated that Dani cried easily and was argumentative. She also stated that Dani began experiencing nightmares and night terrors that included sleep walking. According to mother, Dani's mood fluctuated quickly from sad to angry to happy, and that her primary mood appeared to be anger. She also said that Dani suddenly became "clingy" towards mother, yet would push her away when mother tried to comfort her. Mother indicated that these behaviors were most intense after visits with the father. They decreased throughout the two-weeks between visits and re-escalated after the subsequent paternal visit.

Dani's Troubles Worsen

As the years wore on, mother indicated that Dani's negative behaviors became Dani's primary way of being, regardless of the visitation schedule. Her negative behaviors included stealing, hoarding food, sexually acting out with other children and the family pets, animal mutilation, torture of family pets, and significant attempts to kill the family pets and her younger siblings. According to mother, for the next seven years she was afraid to take Dani out in public because approximately 80% of the time Dani would have an angry episode that included screaming, crying, and rolling around on the floor of the grocery store or throwing food at others in a rage. She would also lie to acquaintances and steal on family outings.

No Help Available

Dani's mother also expressed significant anger at the child welfare system. She knew "something" was wrong with her daughter's behavior and tried getting services when Dani she was five years-old, following the first few visits with her father. Mother said that the human services agencies she reached out to for help thought she was trying to manipulate the system to influence the visitation agreement. In her rural community, Dani's mother believed that people labeled her as a troublesome and/or mentally ill mother. According to mother, mental health professionals initially told her that Dani's behavior resulted from the divorce and that she would stop once she adjusted to it. It became clear to me during the course of this case, that mother's perceptions were accurate about how many of the social service agencies in her county viewed her.

The New Step-Family

When Dani was seven years-old, her mother remarried. She and Dani moved into the home of Dani's stepfather and his five year-old son who happened to have developmental delays. Dani's stepfather was his son's primary caretaker. Dani's stepfather was Caucasian (as was his son) and a stable individual. He provided Dani and her mother with stability in regards to structure and rules.

He worked full time while Dani's mother also worked outside the home. Mother wanted to stay home and be a full time mother to her children, but because of financial difficulties could not afford it. The family was lower middle class, although they owned their own home. Everyone always presented clean and appropriately dressed. The family was highly spiritual and relied on faith to get them through tough times.

Abuse of Siblings and Pets

Dani's mother and stepfather had a child within a year of marrying and a second child a year later. The oldest of these children was a girl and the younger a boy. Although Dani and her mother said that she was excited about the birth of Dani's siblings, she also resented the time they took away from her relationship with her mother. Dani said that within a year, she began trying to hurt them by covering their face with a pillow, placing her hand over their mouth or a knife to their neck (yet never actually cutting or scratching them). This occurred during nap time, unsupervised play times, and at night when Dani was supposed to be asleep. She also did these things to the family pets and the pets of relatives and neighbors.

Only when Dani began acting out in school did the family get some assistance. Dani repeated kindergarten because of behavior-related issues. In the first grade, the school placed her in special education for negative behavior. Although all IQ testing reported Dani in the high average range with little difference between her verbal and performance scores, Dani could not follow simple rules in school and rarely made it through the day without at least one episode of rage that involved hitting, threatening, yelling, screaming, swearing and/or crying. She refused to follow classroom rules, argued continually with the teacher, assaulted other students, and would not complete school work that was well within her capabilities.

During this period, the family began psychiatric services for Dani. Over the years, doctors placed Dani on different medications to address her diagnoses that included Attention Deficit/Hyperactivity Disorder (ADHD), Bi-Polar Disorder, Depression, Anxiety and Oppositional Defiant Disorder (ODD). None of the medications made a difference. The long list of medications Dani used at various times during an eight year period included Ritalin, Concerta, Wellbutrin, Risperdol, Zyprexa, Lithium, Luvox, Remeron, and Triazadone. The family received services from a variety of sources including out-patient counseling services, in-home counseling services, and various volunteer mentors. They also relied heavily on their church for support.

Dani's parents tried most everything to control her behavior. They tried corporal punishments, 1-2-3-Magic, Love and Logic, time-outs, loss of privileges and/or favorite items, groundings, behavior modification, outpatient counseling, in-home individual and family counseling, and psychotroptic medications. Dani's mother also attended various parenting classes and participated in individual therapy to address her issues with parenting a troubled child, her own childhood abuse and neglect, and the after-affects of multiple relationships based in domestic violence.

When Dani began sexually abusing younger children in the community as well as her siblings, she entered the legal system. The county where Dani lived had no foster care homes trained to work with someone with the level of behaviors exhibited by Dani. Hence, Dani was placed in a foster home outside of her county. She resided in the foster home for less than a week before she was caught molesting a younger, foster sibling. Authorities then placed Dani in juvenile detention for four months until they could secure a residential placement for her.

Questions

Now that the author has presented basic information about Dani's life, and before reading on in this case, please perform the following exercises based on your education, experience, the professional literature, and the available best practice evidence. To increase your learning potential, you may want to do this in small groups with other students in your course.

1. Based on the information provided above, construct a three-generation genogram and eco-map that represents Dani's personal, familial, and environmental circumstances. What further information do you need to complete this exercise? What patterns do these two important graphical assessment tools demonstrate?
2. Based on the same information, construct a list of Dani's issues and strengths, drawing from multi-systemic sources.
3. Write a two- to three-page narrative assessment that encompasses Dani's multi-systemic issues and strengths. Review Chapter 1 if necessary. This narrative should provide a comprehensive and multi-systemic explanation of his life as she prepares to undergo treatment with the author. Importantly, what information is missing? What strategies would you use to gain this information from Dani, given her unique history and personal style?
4. Try identifying a theoretical model or approach that you use to guide your assessment. According to the literature, what other theoretical options are available and how would these options change the nature of your assessment?
5. End by developing multi-axial DSM-IV-TR diagnoses for Dani. Provide a list of symptoms that you used to justify you diagnostic decisions. What, if any, information was missing that would make this easier?

Links between Dani and Institutions

One issue that made Dani's case interesting was that the residential program where I worked had close ties with the state-funded mental health agency and the juvenile justice system in Dani's county of origin. Authorities placed Dani on probation and the sexual offenders list for the sexual offenses she committed. She met monthly with her probation officer and attended quarterly review hearings before the judge. I spoke with the probation officer two times per month, keeping him apprised of Dani's progress and setbacks in treatment. Because Dani was a danger in the community, we had to maintain her and the community's safety. This was the major concern of the juvenile justice system. They worried because our residential program was an unlocked facility.

The mental health agency worked with Dani's family for three years prior to her removal and remained involved with the mother, step-father, and siblings by providing psychiatric, family, and individual therapy. I spoke with the family therapist an average of two times per month and together we conducted monthly therapy sessions with the mother and Dani to help them resolve issues between them. We also wanted to keep Dani connected with the therapist from her home county in a positive way since the ultimate goal was for her to return to her county of origin. We decided at the onset of treatment that I would focus my energies on Dani and her needs and do little work with the mother or other family members.

All family treatment would be the responsibility of the family therapist from their county of origin. Although we hoped that Dani would someday return to her family, we all were aware that there was a strong chance this would never occur. Hence, the family therapist worked with Dani's siblings on recovery from the abuse inflicted upon them by Dani, instead of issues pertaining to family reunification.

I also worked with the school that served the residents of Dani's residential program. Dani was clearly a danger and prior to her admission into school; I arranged a meeting with the family therapist, residential program supervisor, residential program school laison, and the director of the residential program. The meeting also included the special education department, principal, and assistant principal of the middle school where she would be assigned to a self-contained class room.

In this meeting, we developed a behavior plan and cleared up communication issues for Dani's treatment. We provided all school personnel with my pager number, along with the residential program school laison in case of emergency. If Dani's behavior became a problem or too disruptive, school personnel could page us to help determine how to help Dani regain control. If this were unsuccessful, we would simply remove her from school for the day.

Theoretical Approach

It was clear that because of the number of agencies working with the family, people in the family in need of treatment, and the severity of problems within the family that a Multiple Systems Model approach would be most helpful. Although the probation officer, the family therapist, and I each took responsibility for specific components of the overall case, we had to remain in close and regular contact and develop healthy working relationships based on professional respect, open communication, and cooperation. Often and unfortunately, this does not happen in joint cases. As Dani's therapist, I decided that making these relationships happen was my responsibility.

A Multiple Systems Model approach understands interactions between and among the various external, family, and internal systems, rather focusing attention solely on any single systemic element. The underlying theme of this model is for the therapist to intervene in the whole system and not treat just one sub-system, such as the offender only (Trepper and Barrett, 1989). I strived to accomplish this throughout the course of treatment.

Interactional Involvement between Dani and her Environment

I gathered my information from Dani, her mother, and the family therapist who had worked closely with Dani and her family for several years prior. As our relationship began, Dani was unwilling to participate in her assessment, treatment planning, and treatment process for the first several months of treatment. She was oppositional to anything I attempted. Dani indicated that she had "no problems," in fact; everyone else was "crazy." She stated that people "lied on her all the time to get her into trouble."

When asked about abusing the younger children, Dani accused them of becoming sexual with her and that she was the actual victim, not them. When I questioned her about the irrational statements she often made to explain current or past inappropriate behaviors, Dani threw a temper tantrum that often resulted in her yelling obscenities while crying and rolling on the floor. Other times, Dani simply walked away and/or threatened them verbally and physically. Yet, while she was housed in the residential program, Dani never actually assaulted a staff person or peer at the center or in school. She certainly threatened attack, but never actually followed through on her threats. Using the strengths perspective, I defined this as progress.

Dani's primary method of interacting with others was through annoying, threatening, oppositional, and/or sexualized behavior. When she entered the program, Dani could not have a conversation with another person. After nearly every conversation, others reported feeling intimidated, annoyed, manipulated, or in some way sexualized by Dani. This included peers and adults. Dani was disallowed contact with anyone more than two years younger than she was. This rule resulted in poor peer relations between Dani and school mates and house mates. Staff was so drained by her needs that they even tried avoiding contact with Dani early in her care. I provided additional education for staff to help them better manage their responses to Dani's often exhausting argumentativeness and untruthfulness. Program staff debriefed after working with her, were encouraged to follow the program rules and behavior modification plan I developed to provide internal and external safety for Dani. The problems with staff dissipated after a short time.

Client Engagement

Dani was initially reluctant to work with me. She tried temper tantrums, threats, tears, self-pity, lies, blaming, yelling, shutting-down, and avoiding as ways to protect herself from engaging in treatment. I sensed that Dani also spent time testing me to see if I could handle her intense anger, hurt, and sadness. The initial testing period lasted six months.

Why did it take so long? In the past, Dani's behaviors worked—people stayed away. Moreover, Dani experienced such intense trauma in her life that she had every right—based on her life experience—to distrust authorities and adults. I believe it would have been foolish to expect otherwise. About all that she ever knew from adults asking for trust was hurt and trauma. Why should she believe that I would be any different?

During the "testing" episode, I "waited out" the problematic behavior that usually lasted anywhere from 15 minutes to the entire session. When her behavior subsided, I moved forward, making sure that her acting out did not get her out of any activities or questions. For example, Dani threw tantrums when I asked her to play the Thinking, Feeling, and Doing Game, when I started a discussion about a particular behavior, and asked her to participate in an art activity. Sometimes she would agree and participate, other times she simply resumed the problematic behavior. After six months of our "dance," she finally realized that I was not afraid of her, that I could handle her emotions, and that the structure of our sessions was not going to change. From then on, Dani did not employ tantrums or threats in sessions. Not until this change occurred, could we begin actually working on the problems and issues that brought her to the residential program originally.

Once Dani felt safe, she began discussing and problem-solving her fears, concerns, and experiences in a healthy way. Initially, this was foreign to her. She had become accustomed to failing to the extent that she could not see herself succeeding at anything, especially therapy. Hence, she would often not try or fall back on maladaptive coping mechanisms that had always worked in the past.

Dani experienced significant levels of shame, defined as "the feeling we have when we evaluate our actions, feelings or behaviors and conclude we have done wrong" (Lewis, 1992). Extreme shame is narcissistic in nature and Dani fulfilled all but one criteria of the narcissistic personality disorder as defined by the DSM IV-TR. Since Dani was not yet 18 years old, I did not list this as a diagnosis. However, this concerned program staff working with Dani.

To develop a better relationship with Dani and to improve her self confidence (she was overweight by 50 pounds), I suggested that we participate in physical activity as part of our work together. Dani selected jogging as our activity. One to two times per week at 7 am, I met Dani for our morning jog. At first, she could not run one city block. By the end of the summer, Dani ran three-quarters of a mile without stopping. She also lost 10 pounds through the exercise. The boost of self confidence helped her better monitor what she ate. This significantly helped our relationship and the quality of her engagement in therapy.

More importantly, she began talking about her insecurities during our morning runs. The distraction of the activity and our improved relationship allowed her to talk about how she felt "abnormal" because she did not think or act similar to other people. She acknowledged that she had not been popular at school since first grade. She wondered aloud why people did not like her. For the first time she was able to express some insight into the issues that brought her to our program.

Sexual Abuse

Approximately one year into treatment, Dani continued denying that anyone had ever sexually abused her. However, she met many of the criteria that would suggest she had been severely sexually abused. As the year wore on, she began saying, "I don't remember being sexually abused" when the issue occasionally came up in girls group, family, or individual therapy. Earlier, she would emphatically state, "I wasn't sexually abused." This change of language further led me to believe that she had been abused, but that she was fearful of disclosing this information.

Because of her history of using manipulative coping skills, I carefully questioned her in this area to ensure that I did not ask leading questions about sexual abuse. If Dani disclosed her abuse history, I wanted it to be through her initiative, not because she was telling me something she thought I wanted to hear. I believed that if I pressured her to disclose a sexual abuse history that she would resent the pressure and never disclose the abuse or disclose the abuse and then refuse to discuss it. We needed to get to this issue honestly and on her terms.

About the time we were delving into sexual abuse for the first time, Dani's mother found her two youngest children having sex when they were supposed to be napping. The older child indicated that she had learned how to do this from Dani. This was new information, since Dani had previously disclosed that she had "only" fondled the kids. Because Dani was involved in the legal system and this disclosure could result in additional charges, I told Dani about her sister's disclosure.

Dani immediately admitted to having performed this sexual act (oral sex) as well as others on both her younger siblings. She then blurted out (this is the best description of how she disclosed) that her father had performed oral sex on her and had done "lots of other stuff." As we talked, she shared that she could not tell anyone because her dad had threatened to harm her younger half-siblings and her mother. He even went so far as to kill one of her pets in front of Dani to assure her that bad things would happen if she ever told anyone about the abuse. Although her father was deceased, she continued to fear that he would harm her and those that she loved. Over the next several months, she revealed more about her abuse including forced oral, anal, and vaginal sex, sex with half siblings as father watched, forced viewing of pornography, voyeuristic behavior where the father would have sex with an adult female in front of Dani, and aspects of torture and sadism.

Similar to many sexual abuse victims, Dani believed she "killed" her father because she often "wished" him dead. Based on this, I believed that Dani was "stuck" in the Toddler Stage of Erikson's Stages of Development. Because of the trauma of abuse, Dani never completed Erikson's task of Autonomy vs. Shame. In this stage, children master the physical environment and simultaneously maintain their sense of self-esteem. A component of this phase is magical thinking, a phenomenon where children believe something will happen just because they thought about it. Other factors that suggested she was "stuck" in this phase of development included, an undeveloped healthy sense of control, aggression, and a lack of initiative with peers.

Questions _____

1. **Compare the assessment and diagnoses developed with the Author's assessment. What differences and similarities do you notice? What are the ramifications for treatment demonstrated by the differences between the two assessments?**

2. Based on your assessment and diagnoses, develop a multi-systemic treatment plan for Dani that encompasses the information contained in your multi-systemic assessment. Include short and long-term goals in your treatment plan.
3. Based on your assessment and treatment plan, what treatment theory, and/or combination of theories do you believe best fits Dani and her reality? What specific interventions would you use if you were assigned to work with Dani? Defend your decisions.

Treatment Planning: Decision-Making and Negotiation

As I discussed earlier, my early work with Dani was limited because of her inability to trust and fear of change. As she learned to trust that I would not harm her, Dani invested in her treatment. I informed her early on that my initial goal was to help her stop sexually hurtful and homicidal behaviors so that she did not end up in a long-term detention center for youth and ultimately, prison. Dani's initial reaction was to deny that she had ever hurt anyone. However, since she knew this was not true, and knew that I believed she had done these things, I kept the goal the same. I made this decision contrary to the tenets of Person Centered Therapy, an approach that I generally use with clients.

Person Center Therapy, based on a subjective view of human experience, emphasizes client resources for becoming aware and resolving blocks to personal growth. It places clients, and not therapists, at the center of therapy (Corey, 1991). That is, according to Person Centered Therapy, I should have changed the treatment goal to match Dani's desires at the time.

I also focused on Dani's strengths, looking for ways to use them in treatment. First, Dani had no history of suicidal ideation or attempts. Second, Dani was a bright child who read and wrote well and had the intellectual capacity to learn. Third, she had a supportive family that wanted contact with her and wanted her to get healthy and be part of their family. Fourth, she had tremendous drive and energy. I believed that if we could alter the course of her personal energies from self-destructive to self-supportive so she could heal.

Because of her probation officer's desire to send her to a long-term detention facility, if Dani had one more incident of harmful behavior she would be immediately removed from our treatment program. Since Dani was intelligent, I knew that even if she argued with me on this issue she understood the probation officer's fear about her harming others in the future. Everyone in her life had explained this to her. Dani could verbalize that this was her "last chance" and that if she "messed up" she was going to be in a locked facility for a long time. Although she disliked rules, she disliked the idea of rules in a locked setting even more. While Dani broke lesser rules everyday, she knew the limit (harming others) and when to stop. This suggested that despite her claim to having no control over self, Dani actually had considerable control than most people gave her credit for or that she realized.

During Dani's stay in residential treatment, she participated in individual, group, family, and activity therapy. More importantly, she participated in atypical treatment time the direct care staff and me. I discuss the atypical treatment later in this section.

Individual Therapy

I had a simple, yet difficult initial goal in individual therapy—engage Dani in treatment. Dani did not want any part of treatment. She clearly stated that she did not want to change. When Dani entered the program, she reported that she had been "in charge" of her life until recently and she wanted that control back. At the same time, Dani knew that if she did not change, she would end up in a locked placement, something she truly feared. I finally engaged Dani in therapy by utilizing atypical therapy approaches. As stated earlier, we regularly ran together. This let her know that I would do something she wanted to do and that I would follow through with our seven am meetings to reinforce structure and safety.

I also made it a point to attend her court and family therapy sessions. This allowed us to spend time together in the car for at least six hours per monthly round trip. During these trips, I provided Dani the individual attention she craved. We played typical road games (spell the alphabet using letters in road signs), listened to music she enjoyed, and talked about many things, some treatment related and others not. During our tips, Dani often brought up first time concerns about peer and staff interactions on these trips.

One of the pitfalls of residential treatment is that all the residents vie for attention from the staff. If they do not receive attention directly, residents often act out to achieve their goal, leaving residents who are doing well with considerably less attention. Hence, these trips provided Dani a dose of individualized, positive attention that she utilized in a healthy manner. She looked forward to our trips and planned for them to get the most from it. For example, Dani would find out which staff person was going with us beforehand. She would select music to listen to ahead of time, bring a book to read sections aloud to us, and/or bring a craft that we could work on in the car. She planned these events with our interests in mind. This was one of her first consistent efforts to meet the needs of others. Inevitably, staff would report a better working relationship with Dani after a trip.

Once Dani invested in treatment, individual work focused on a variety of topics. The overriding issue was safety for the community and safety for Dani. We developed our treatment goals and objectives to meet this requirement. This case was challenging mainly because of the number of issues and high stakes for the community if Dani re-offended. When I developed her treatment plan with input from the staff, I often became overwhelmed with the many concerns we had regarding Dani's multiple negative behaviors. As a therapist, I first had to narrow what behaviors to focus on for the safety of the community. Dani's first treatment goal was as follows:

Goal: Dani will stop physically harming others.
Objectives:
1. Dani will have no sexual contact with others.
2. Dani will hurt people through hitting, kicking, or other physical means
3. Dani will talk to her therapist, program supervisor, her mentor, or a staff person if she has the desire to act out sexually or assault anyone.

Dani did not want to work on this goal. She said that these issues were not problems for her. However, we all knew better. Pertaining to this goal, instead of a person centered approach I used a Relapse Prevention Approach that believes sex offenses are not impulsive acts, but the culmination of processes that build over time (Barbaree, Marshall, & Hudson, 1993). Dani's sexually hurtful behavior was not impulsive, but carefully planned and carried out. She controlled her actions. That is, she waited until she knew she would get away with the behaviors. This behavior fit with the relapse prevention model discussed above.

I developed and maintained this initial goal to let her know that this was important. Moreover, making this our first goal communicated why she was in the program and laid the foundation for the remainder of her treatment. This goal also indirectly confronted Dani's denial regarding the dangerousness of her behaviors. It also communicated to Dani that she was both a victim of sexual abuse and responsible for victimizing others through sexual abuse.

To help her reach this goal, we developed a stringent behavior modification plan that involved immediate rewards for positive behavior and immediate consequences for negative behavior. We developed our plan in collaboration with Dani to offer her some control aimed at getting her to "buy into" the program. Interestingly, Dani suggested consequences for herself that were harsh and illegal, even for minor infractions. We worked with Dani to learn the difference between minor and serious infractions.

At first, Dani tested the rules numerous times. She purposely isolated herself with a younger peer, identified younger boys (in the 5 to 8 year old range) as her boyfriend, left the program without permission, obtained pornographic material, failed to maintain personal boundaries with others, and exhibited openly intimidating or sexualized behaviors with younger siblings. These behaviors all fit her pattern of sexually hurtful behavior. With each incident, Dani became enraged when we imposed consequences. She would yell obscenities, make threats such as, "I'm gonna cut that baby out of your belly," and commit further infractions in front of staff to provoke a response.

I also began working with Dani on sexually acting out in coordination with her sex offender girl's group assignments. We began by identifying the offense chain that she used when sexually harming others and ways to stop sexually hurtful behaviors. Recall that during the initial phase of treatment, Dani admitted to some sexualized behaviors (fondling over and under the clothes). Because she admitted to some sexually inappropriate behaviors, I could begin working on this issue directly. Dani minimized her behaviors and often blamed the survivors, stating that they forced her to have sex with them or that they had conducted themselves in a sexually provocative manner towards her. Her denial made it initially difficult to make progress. Whenever we addressed the issue, Dani exhibited distorted thinking, denial, and blaming the victim. Each time, I calmly addressed each maladaptive coping mechanism that she used to justify the sexual assaults. Eventually, Dani did this herself.

After the first six months, Dani began making progress. She verbalized her acceptance pf the first treatment goal during an individual session and later that month in a family session. While I am not sure she was ready to change, I believe Dani realized that her current coping mechanisms did not work and she needed new skills. During this family session, we added another goal to Dani's treatment plan. The breakthrough occurred when Dani suggested the next treatment goal.

> **Goal:** I will be nicer to people
> **Objectives:**
>
>   1. I will not yell at people
>   2. I will not swear at people
>   3. I will not trick people into doing what I want them to do
>   4. I will not be so grumpy all the time

This goal marked significant progress. By saying she wanted to work at being nicer, Dani acknowledged that she needed to change and not others. She took the first step towards accepting responsibility for her actions.

This particular session marked a turnaround in Dani's treatment. We had been tracking certain behaviors to monitor her progress, including irritable outbursts (yelling, crying, arguing), threatening outbursts (threatening to physically harm someone), sexualized behaviors (isolating, sexual talk at or with a peer), annoying behaviors (ignoring staff, teasing peers), and assaults.

Over this period, Dani did not assault anyone while a resident of the program. She exhibited sexualized behavior an average of 1.5 times per week, threatening behavior two times per month, irritable behavior six times per day and annoying behaviors seven times per day. After she suggested to "work on being nice to people," all the behaviors decreased except the sexualized behaviors. Although the annoying, threatening, and irritable behaviors continued to occur, they occurred about half as often. This led us to believe that Dani was engaged in treatment. The sexualized behaviors unfortunately did not decrease at this time. This suggested that these behaviors were even more significant in her life that we initially believed.

As Dani progressed, we added additional goals and objectives.

> **Goal:** Dani will learn relapse prevention skills
> **Objectives:**
>
>   1. Dani will complete her own cycle of abuse wheel
>   2. Dani will complete the relapse prevention workbook
>   3. Dani will complete the female adolescent sex offender group
>   4. Dani will identify how her own sexual abuse relates to her sexually hurtful behaviors of others.

This goal went to the "heart" of her treatment. That is, if Dani was to cease sexually abusing others, she needed to examine and explore her own abuse and how it contributed to the abuse of others. Hence, I saw this as the most important goal for Dani's treatment, and future life.

Goal: Improve relations with peer group
Objectives:
1. Dani will make two friends at school
2. Dani will decrease annoying behaviors to one per day
3. Dani will learn to develop and maintain friendships

Dani stated early in treatment that people did not like her, and that she had no friends since first grade. For her to be successful in life, Dani needed to learn how to make and maintain non-sexualized friendships. This goal addressed this important issue directly.

Additionally, we used short term, targeted behavior modification plans and increased structure to deal with new behaviors as they occurred. Some of the issues we had to deal with included superficial gang and cult involvement, threatening to run away from the program, hoarding food, clothing and craft supplies, stealing, poor hygiene, and excessive masturbatory behaviors.

Group Therapy

Dani participated in a twice-weekly group therapy that focused on her relationships with peers. By definition, residential programs see a variety of unhealthy behaviors. Because of her irritability and poor social skills, Dani became a target for teasing, exclusion, and tattling by her peers. She accurately determined that most of her peers did not like her. Through group therapy (and other "house meetings") Dani received and eventually acted on feedback from peers about her behavior. This was a painful process for Dani, as her peer's issues were not always presented diplomatically or with empathy. After these groups, Dani would process her feelings with me about peer feedback. Although group was uncomfortable, and sometimes hurtful, it taught her to handle criticism, begin separating when the issue was about her, and how to respond appropriately when others are angry. Group also taught her to give others feedback in an assertive (and not aggressive) aggressive manner.

Family Therapy

Family Therapy focused on Dani and her mother's relationship. They had a long history of not getting along when together, but missing each other when apart. This dynamic really took center stage once Dani entered treatment. Previously, her mother told the professionals that Dani needed to be removed from the home because they were all in danger. Once Dani was removed, her mother did a turn around and immediately wanted Dani returned home. Often, incestuous families "appear to live in an all or nothing world and cannot conceive of life in shades of gray. This is one reason why enmeshed families may fluctuate between enmeshed and disengaged" (Trepper and Barrett, 1989, p. 33). This paradox confused Dani and initially provided false hopes that she would not have to complete the program.

Together with the family therapist, I worked with Dani and her mother to re-define their relationship and their family structure. We addressed mother and Dani's belief that the other was emotionally dependent and would cease to exist if separated.

We also directly said that we did not expect the family to reunite. The best we hoped for was for Dani to enter a long-term foster home after completing the residential program. Initially, Dani and her mother resisted. However, as the extent of Dani's sexual abusive behavior surfaced in the younger children, mother agreed that foster care was the best plan. Additionally, once separated from her mother, Dani enjoyed not feeling that she needed to fulfill her mother's emotional needs. Knowing her mother could take care of herself allowed Dani to concentrate on her needs in a healthier way.

Because of Dani's sexualized behavior with her siblings during family visits, we limited visits to her mother and step-father. At first, we believed that Dani would react poorly to this rule. However, to our surprise Dani said she was relieved. She stated that when they arrived, she found herself repeating old behaviors and did not feel that she had sufficient control over her impulses around them. For the duration of therapy, the siblings did not visit Dani again. The family therapist indicated that as therapy progressed, the younger children did not want to see Dani because they finally felt safe enough to express their anger with her.

Dani also attended group therapy for adolescent, sexually abused females. This group became invaluable in her treatment. She was in group with other girls that did exactly what she did to younger children. This open-ended group was assignment focused. Each client had 10 written assignments to complete during the group, at their own pace. Some group members were done in a year, while others took three years. Dani completed her final assignment two years into treatment. Graduation from the residential program was contingent upon completion of the adolescent sex offender group. After each group member completed an assignment and presented it to their peers. Peers provided Dani with feedback and told about the changes that needed to occur in the assignment.

It is typical for group members to be "stuck" on one particular assignment for several weeks or months. Dani was able to breeze through the first several assignments because she was bright and a good writer. Dani struggled with the assignment on empathy. Her peers saw through her fancy words and sentences. She tried to make it as long as possible (more than a typewritten page) in an effort to fool them into thinking she understood the concept. It did not work. The group kept refusing to pass her on the assignment. Her frustration was evidenced by her attempts to manipulate circumstances so that she did not have to attend the group and expressing hostility toward group members when the provided her feed back.

Although she could define empathy using a dictionary, Dani did not feel empathy and was unable to express it with any honesty. She was stuck on this assignment for five months. She presented it six times during that five month period. As she experienced the safety and consistency of the residential program, Dani began looking at the needs of others and not just her. She connected with what it must have been like for the survivors of her sexual abuse after she disclosed how her father had sexually abused her. This breakthrough allowed Dani to move on and graduate from the group.

Therapeutic Recreation

Two times per week, Dani participated in therapeutic recreations (TR), defined as a process that utilizes recreation services for intervention in some physical, emotional and/or social behavior to bring about a desired change and promote individual growth and development (Peterson and Gunn, 1984). During RT, Dani's specific goals focused on developing pro-social skills and improved confidence in her physical skills. These goals were critical to her success.

She had gained (and at times lost) significant amounts of weight over the years because of the many psychotropic medications she took. During her stay in the program, Dani took Zyprexa for anger management, Lithium and Wellbutrin for mood management. At one point, she took Remeron for anxiety and Concerta for attention related issues. She also took Triazadone on an as needed basis to help her sleep. During the first six months of treatment, she gained more than 50 pounds. This devastated her since she had been only slightly above average weight prior to entering the program. We suspected that her weight gain was due in part to the side effects of the medications and self-soothing behavior of overeating. She said that she had to eat for "something to do" when she felt empty inside. I also suspected that she ate more to get "bigger," to become more intimidating to staff and peers. If people were not afraid of her at 130 pounds, they might afraid at 180 pounds. Regardless, the weight gain and accompanying body image problems became a treatment issue.

Through RT, Dani began swimming, biking, lifting weights and doing aerobics. These activities were a regular part of her treatment and not "rewards" for good behavior. RT also introduced Dani to team-building exercises, confidence building exercises (such as a high ropes course), and physical confidence-building exercises. At first, Dani resisted RT. By the end of treatment, she became proficient at swimming, understood her body in relation to others, and took leadership roles in team-building activities.

RT also helped Dani to identify non-hurtful ways to occupy her leisure time. In the past, Dani spent considerable time focused on hurtful or vengeful fantasies while excluding other activities. Because she was considered a "child with problems" in her home county, other families did not want their children spending time with her. This left her with a lot of time to fill. Because her unhealthy fantasies filled the need for immediate gratification, Dani ceased participation in other activities, such as reading, crafts, games, physical activities, etc. Dani also filled "down time" with unhealthy amounts of masturbatory activities. As she began developing new interests, the number of times she masturbated per day also decreased.

Questions

Now that the author has discussed the treatment plan she developed for Dani, compare the treatment plan used in the case with the treatment plan you developed earlier.

1. **In what ways does your treatment plan differ from the authors? Please develop an informed critique of the authors plan, and include the reasons you agree or disagree with the author's choices.**
2. **What do the differences between treatment plans imply for treatment in this case?**

Ethical Challenges

The greatest of this case involved balancing community safety against Dani's treatment needs. Throughout treatment, Dani exhibited behaviors she exhibited while sexually abusing. She also exhibited new behaviors not previously observed and verbalized thoughts and feelings she had during therapy that clearly suggested she was at risk to re-offend. The primary goal with juvenile sex offenders is to protect the community. Each time we observed an increase in her sexually hurtful pattern, we increased the structure to ensure safety. The most difficult decision regarding this issue occurred when we had to decide if Dani could leave treatment and re-enter the community.

We knew that we were accepting a challenge, since Dani would attend public school and be able to "walk out the door" of the program if she chose. We had to weigh the risks. From her history, we knew that Dani had never run away from home or school. In her life, she rarely hid from school personnel or parents and never left altogether.

Additionally, Dani indicated that she was afraid of the "city" and felt that if she left the program she would get hurt. Her fear of the city never dissipated during her treatment. Finally, Dani was a bright girl who we suspected had been severely and chronically traumatized. We decided that if we could address those issues, her negative acting out would decrease significantly.

The second ethical challenge that arose during the course of treatment was how to deal with Dani's disclosure of her own sexual abuse. This was tricky because the reason she was in the program was to address how she abused others. I decided to acknowledge the abuse, but not to make that the focus of her treatment. The primary goal in treatment was to ensure that she did not re-offend.

By abandoning the relapse prevention model to focus on her own victimization, I would have left Dani without the tools she needed to ensure she did not re-offend. Since we maintained a close working relationship with her family therapist, I decided that the family therapist would reinforce the relapse prevention strategies and begin working with Dani on her own victimization after her discharge from the residential program and into a foster care home.

Questions _____

The author presented two ethical issues she considered in this case: protecting the community and delaying treatment for her abuse to focus on relapse prevention. Before moving on, consider the following.

1. What is your opinion of the author's presentation of the issues? Examine the code of professional ethics in your profession and the current practice literature regarding these subjects. What could the author have done differently? What would you do differently if you worked with a client such as Dani?
2. What other potential ethical issues are generated by this case? Explain the issues and explicate how you would address whatever ethical issues you discover in this case.

3. **Regarding the decision about her ability to re-enter the community after treatment, what is your opinion on this issue? Examine the professional literature regarding sexual offenders and their treatment success rate. Given the information learned in your literature search, on what grounds would you be able to make an informed decision to terminate her treatment successfully? Is it possible? What would you say was Dani's prognosis for post-treatment success?**

Termination

After two years, we terminated Dani from residential treatment successfully. In our judgment, Dani met all of her treatment goals in this time. I must stress that successful termination in this case does not mean that Dani was "cured." I could not guarantee that Dani would not sexually abuse harm again. It would be unethical and impossible to ensure another person's behavior. I did believe that Dani learned healthier coping techniques and her risk to re-offend greatly decreased.

If you recall Dani's treatment goals, she made significant progress on the first goal of relapse prevention. By the time she graduated, Dani had not sexually acted out or acted provocatively in five months. In addition, she never assaulted anyone during the course of her treatment and had not threatened to assault anyone in four months. Finally, she utilized her therapist, staff, and mentors to help solve problems in healthy ways.

Dani worked hard on her goal to be nicer to people, but made less progress than on goal one. Although she made progress, Dani continued struggling with an overall feeling of irritability. Life's little annoyances created havoc for her in daily life. Minor changes in plans or waiting her turn continued to be issues. Although these behaviors made it difficult for Dani and those around her, she tried to make changes. Dani was aware that her irritability was an issue and agreed to continue working on this issue. Although medication seemed to alleviate some of her irritability, it was clearly not the sole answer to this problem.

Goal three about her victimization was the "nuts and bolts" of her treatment if she were to stop abusing others. Dani made good progress toward this goal. She completed all five objectives. Her next step will be to continue examining this painful issue in her life during aftercare with the family therapist.

Pertaining to goal four and making friends, Dani made excellent progress. When Dani graduated, she had three friends at her school, beating her goal of two friends. Even more significant was that she maintained these friendships for nearly six months. She said that this was the first time in her life that she actually had friends her age. Because of her irritability, Dani did not make friends in the residential program. However, I saw this as positive since we wanted her to make friendships with healthy people and not with troubles kids.

Dani's annoying behavior decreased to none at school. This signaled significant progress. When she first joined the program, the school called us several times per week to address her acting out behaviors. By the time she graduated, Dani's teachers reported positive social skills and leadership skills in the classroom. Dani made the honor role for the first time during her first semester. School personnel also discussed placing her in resource room, out of the self-contained classroom. This became an additional motivating factor for Dani to maintain appropriate behavior at school, since she was well aware of the stigma attached to special education classes.

Aftercare Plans

Upon graduation, Dani returned to her home county. The mental health agency and her probation officer found a foster care home to meet her specialized needs. This two-parent, foster family was provided training about sexually hurtful behaviors, were unable to take other children for at least one year, and were provided security measures (alarms on doors, etc.) to help ensure safety. In addition, Dani transitioned slowly into their home starting with day visits and working up to overnight visits on week-ends.

Equally as important, the family therapist never stopped working with Dani and her family. When Dani returned to her home county, she knew that she was returning to a therapist that she had worked with in the past. This was important for Dani, since she did not like telling new people her story. She understood that the family therapist knew the details of her life and how she had harmed others.

We talked about discharge long before it occurred and Dani agreed that when she graduated from the residential program she would begin working on her own issues of victimization. This transition plan worked well, ensuring that Dani had structure in place before she left the structure of the residential placement.

Questions _____

The author presented an interesting, successfully terminated case that involved many issues commonly found in practice with sexual abuse cases and others that are not so common. Taking a broad view of this case, reevaluate the author's work and your participation through the questions asked throughout the case.

1. **Review Dani's progress in treatment. Based on the author's description, the professional literature, and the latest practice evidence, what occurred to account for Dani's progress?**
2. **What was the theoretical approach or combination of approaches that appeared to work best for Dani? What will happen to Dani when she leaves the structured, behavioral modification environment of the residential facility to a home and life where rewards and consequences are not immediately forthcoming? To assist with this question, examine the professional and practice literature about the success of behavioral modification programs post treatment. What does the literature say about this type of program?**
3. **What additional intervention(s) would you recommend? Use the professional literature and latest practice evidence to justify your recommendations.**

4. Overall, what is your professional opinion of the work performed in this case? As always, refer to the professional literature, practice evidence, your experience, and the experience of peers when developing your opinion.

5. Based on your review, what additional or alternative approaches could the author have used with Dani? That is, if you were the practitioner, how would you have approached this case? Please explain and justify your approach.

6. What did the case demonstrate that you could use in other practice settings? List the most important issues you learned and their relevance in your future practice career.

Bibliography

Barbaree, H. E, Marshall, W. L., & Hudson, S. M. (1993). *The juvenile sex offender*. New York: The Guilford Press.

Corey, G. (1991). *Manual for theory and practice of counseling and psychotherapy*. Pacific Grove, CA: Brooks/Cole.

Lewis, M. (1992). *Shame, the exposed self*. New York: The Free Press.

Peterson, C. A., & Gunn, S. L. (1984). *Therapeutic recreation program design*. Englewood Cliffs, NJ: Prentice Hall.

Trepper, T. S., & Barrett, M. J. (1989). *Systematic treatment of incest. A therapeutic handbook*. Bristol, PA: Brunner/Mazel.

5

Mary

Cathy Simmons

Mary's case is an excellent example of the many issues clients with co-occurring disorders face, including chaotic family systems, sexual abuse; domestic violence, self-defeating behaviors, and multiple substance relapses. These are only a few of the practice issues presented in this case.

Dual or multi-diagnosed clients present significant challenges to practitioners. Although clients often present with one primary problem, rarely do they have only one issue (Shulman, 1999). In fact, some believe that most clients fit in the category of the dually or multi-diagnosed (Johnson, 2004). Layers of dysfunction, hidden problems, and multiple co-occurring disorders often exist in many (if not most) cases (Shulman, 1999). Mary's case provides readers the chance to explore a person with co-occurring disorders and think about how they would handle similar situations in practice.

Mary: The Assessment Process

Mary scheduled an appointment for a substance abuse assessment after her release from jail. She was arrested for Driving While Intoxicated (DWI). The police stopped her for running a red light and arrested her when the officer detected alcohol on her breath. I met her the next day for an assessment appointment at our multi-disciplinary outpatient mental health and substance abuse clinic. Our clinic provides short and long-term counseling to individuals and families with a variety of mental health and substance abuse concerns. When she made the appointment, Mary stated that she wanted help with her drinking and perhaps other problems too. However, drinking was her primary concern and became her presenting problem.

Typically, initial appointments consist of a biopsychosocial assessment that includes gathering and assessing information regarding a client's spirituality, family of origin, family of creation, medical concerns, mental health history, childhood and adult abuse history, substance use, current symptoms, duration of problems, coping skills, and social supports. From the beginning, Mary was forthcoming about her life; clearly stating that she believed her drinking was "out of control." It was impossible to determine at this early stage whether Mary was motivated to change, or simply frightened into an appointment to help with her upcoming legal problems.

Multi-Systematic Assessment Information

Demographic Information

Mary was a 33-year-old, overweight Caucasian woman working as an assistant manager in a greeting card store. She was five-foot four-inches (5' 4") tall with long brown hair and sunken, green eyes. Although she wore neatly pressed slacks and dresses to work, she usually came to therapy in sweat clothes with her hair pulled back. Someone looking at her for the first time might describe Mary as "dumpy." However, when she smiled, it was easy to see that Mary was an attractive woman.

Mary was self-conscious about her appearance. When we first met, she claimed that her physical appearance was "horrible" and she rarely made eye contact. She had trouble accepting complements in any form, replying to kind words dismissively. Beyond her appearance, Mary talked as if she was a worthless person with no redeeming qualities. I sensed that it never occurred to her that she had any positive qualities. I was unsure if I had ever met someone with a lower self-image that Mary demonstrated during our first appointment.

According to Mary, people in her life did not say kind things to her without becoming sarcastic and critical during the conversation. For example, according to Mary, when people said, "nice dress," they really mean that it was ugly or they were setting her up for a bigger criticism such as "but it's not nice on you." Criticism or "dissin," as Mary called it had been her reality since her childhood. Starting early in life, other people's sarcasm fed her low self-image, serving to shape her sullen disposition and low self-worth.

Mary always had a weight problem. She grew up an overweight child with few friends. Often overlooked by teachers, she earned "average" grades and did not participate in after-school activities. In fact, she spent most of her life trying to hide from everyone in social situations. Regarding her childhood, Mary recalls mostly painful experiences. For example, she talked about the constant teasing she suffered by other children and having to eat lunch alone at school.

As a child, Mary believed she was ugly, dumb, and worthless. She also learned, or perceived, that people did not like her, including her parents. Her parents cemented these beliefs by regularly criticizing her and using sarcasm as their main method communication. Mary recalled countless occasions when her parents called her abusive names such as "fat," "stupid," and "ugly." She also remembered not knowing when to believe or trust the kind words of others. According to Mary, "you just never know if they're being serious." From childhood, other people's hurtful words affected every aspect of Mary's life, playing a significant role in the development of her low self-concept and her "worthless" adult identity.

Mary's Coping Mechanisms

As a result, Mary developed (and continues using) three primary coping mechanisms: a baseline low mood, overeating, and lately, excessive alcohol use. Her low mood contained symptoms such as low self-esteem, feelings of hopelessness, low energy, overeating, recurrent, dull headaches, and sleep problems, consisting mainly of problems falling asleep and nightmares. Her symptoms were not always present in the same degree and were variable over the years. Although she never experienced a major depressive episode, her baseline mood was consistently low and had been for many years ("As long as I can remember").

While her symptoms had a negative impact on her life, they also served a protective function. Beginning in adolescence, Mary's chronic low mood and negative outlook protected her from becoming hurt and disappointed. That is, by being unhappy and sullen most of the time, Mary never worried about being let down by people in her life. As Mary stated, "The rug won't ever be pulled out from under me" because she never expected much from people.

Mary's second long term coping mechanism involved chronic overeating. Mary used food as both a comfort and a "friend." Fighting a lifelong battle with obesity, Mary's excessive weight functioned as a shield against the cruelty of others. It also served as a cause for their cruelty as well. Throughout her life, people teased her incessantly and treated her poorly because of her weight. As a result, Mary ate to compensate for the pain she felt about her appearance, worthlessness, treatment by others, and her inability to "fit in." The double-edged sword eating brought to Mary's life played a significant role in her developing personal identity, self-image, and experiences as an adult. Being obese in Western society has significant negative connotations in how people view themselves in relation to others, and how others view the overweight. Mary's experience reflected this statement.

The third coping mechanism Mary began using more recently involved alcohol abuse. She reported drinking since adolescence, yet in the last year or so she began drinking heavily and daily. Drinking had become a routine part of her life. Mary said that she often went to work drunk or with a hangover. According to Mary, excessive drinking helped her cope with low mood, family changes, and her difficult past. Additionally, alcohol was a comfort and numbing agent related to her daily stress, pain from childhood, and her inability to make friends.

Specifically, Mary reported having problems at work related to drinking. In fact, she suspected that her boss believed that she had a drinking problem. She also admitted to driving to work on a number of occasions with hangovers or still intoxicated from the night before. Moreover, Mary stated that she had frequent arguments with her husband and eldest son while drinking. Mary further admitted that despite the problems caused by drinking, she continued drinking on a daily basis.

Further, Mary stated that she did not remember the last time she drank less than a full bottle of wine during the night. Over the previous year, a typical evening entailed drinking a glass of wine preparing dinner, a second with dinner, and the remainder of the bottle before going to bed. Recently, she would finish the first bottle and drink a second to help her fall asleep. Mary said she only drank wine and never "hard liquor." She also stated that it now takes more alcohol for her to get the same effect as she used to feel drinking less.

Socially, Mary reported suffering throughout most of her life. She said that people did not like her and were often harsh in how they treated her. Hence, the negative stereotyping and resultant words and actions of others exacerbated her compensatory eating and intensified her low mood and alcohol use. Her life was bound-up in a never-ending cycle of low mood, overeating, and alcohol use, each of which served several functions in her life and had caused her tremendous pain and disruption since childhood.

Questions _____

Before moving on, examine the professional literature regarding the linkages between addictive behavior (alcohol & food), childhood sexual abuse, and domestic violence.

1. **What does the literature say about these issues? Does the literature point to any linkages in people's lives?**
2. **If so, what does the practice literature suggest as the most effective ways of engaging clients presenting with some combination of these issues in their lives?**

Family of Origin: The Beginning

Raised by her biological parents with a younger brother, Mary grew up in a small town in the Northeast United States. She described her childhood as "hard." Both of her parents had significant drinking problems. According to Mary, her family was chaotic and parents out of control. Her parents drank daily, argued, and fought regularly, often resulting in physical violence between them and sometimes involving the children. Her parents drank heavily every weekend and often during the week. She stated that they often drank to the point of passing out and always experienced painful hangovers.

Mary remembered that her father was "in and out of work," primarily employed as a carpenter but took whatever work he could find. To make ends meet, her mother (Nancy) frequently worked part-time jobs as a server in different bars and restaurants. She remembered that the family always had financial problems and rarely paid their bills on time. Life was a struggle in Mary's family from the beginning.

Mary believed that her parents loved each other, "they just had a hard time showing it." Routine parental arguments routinely turned violent. Mary said that her parents often hit each other and broke things (e.g. dishes, mirrors, walls, etc.). Sometimes they involved Mary and her younger brother in their fights, but usually the two siblings "just stayed out of their way." The police often came to the house and arrested her father during their arguments and fights. He always returned home the following day after a night in the "tank." Nancy always dropped charges and told Mary that this was how marriage worked.

Mary witnessed domestic violence and was the victim (survivor) of physical and emotional abuse as a child. She recalled her father and mother hitting her on numerous occasions during their drunken evenings. Her parents also emotionally abused Mary, saying "mean things" about her appearance, primarily about her weight.

Possible Sexual Abuse

Given her family history and the prevalence of sexual abuse in chaotic and otherwise abusive families with alcoholic members (Johnson, 2004), I asked Mary whether she had ever been sexually abused as a child. At first, she denied any sexual abuse. However, her body language, affect, and certain symptoms discussed earlier led me to believe that she might have withheld the truth. Perhaps she blocked these memories. More likely, it was too early in our relationship for her to reveal this fact. It was also possible that it never happened. However, my instincts and experience suggested that her father, family friends, or others probably abused her. I decided to postpone this line of questioning for a while, hoping to build the level of trust between us that would allow her to be forthright about her past.

Excusing the abuse she did discuss, Mary stated that it was always "caused by the alcohol." Mary had a hard time accepting that she was abused as a child and that her parents were the abusers. She found it even more difficult to accept that her parents would hurt her without an excuse ("they had to be drunk . . . it was not their fault"). Several times, she stated that when her parent's were sober, "they were wonderful people." However, when talking about specific incidents of abuse, her nonverbal behavior clearly indicated painful memories and lingering trauma, perhaps far deeper than she admitted during our first session.

Questions _____

In the paragraphs above, the author stated that she sensed that someone sexually abused Mary as a child. She cited an instinct based on knowledge and experience. However, the author also mentioned that her hunch was based on several of Mary's other presented symptoms and various issues in her family of origin. Based on these statements, please consider the following before moving on in this case.

1. Examine the literature on sexual abuse, especially pertaining to adult survivors of sexual abuse. What signs and symptoms does the literature cite as being important in suspecting and identifying sexual abuse from childhood?

2. **What does the practice literature suggest is the best way to approach adult clients about childhood sexual abuse? What strategies could the author use to engage Mary around this sensitive and personal subject? Does the literature cite any differences in these strategies based on the gender and/or age of clients?**

3. **Further, examine the literature about the controversial topic of repressed memories in adult clients. Over the years, researchers and practitioners have attacked and defended repressed memory syndrome passionately. What is the current belief system pertaining to the existence of repressed memory syndrome? Discuss and debate this issue among your peers in a small group or classroom setting.**

Changes and Disruptions

When Mary was 16 years old, her family changed. Her father died suddenly in an alcohol related car accident after years of serious alcoholism. Beyond the grief of losing a father and husband, he left the family no life insurance or savings to help them live. Hence, the loss of his income forced the family's dependence on welfare and Social Security. Although her mother tried to make ends meet for a few months, the income she earned was not sufficient to pay the bills. At 16 years-old, Mary dropped out of high school and began working as a grocery store clerk to help the family.

Mary said that she did not regret dropping out of high school. Instead, she reported feeling proud of her ability to help take care of the family at such a young age. In addition, Mary continued shouldering enormous responsibility for her mother, despite the hardship it brings to her life and family.

Family of Origin—Current Situation

Since the time of her father's death, Mary was her mother's (Nancy's) primary support and caretaker. Although Nancy had income from social security and a part-time job, her heavy drinking and overall poor decision-making consistently exhausted Nancy's finances and patience.

At the time of our first session, Nancy lived with Mary. The financial support Mary gave to Nancy caused significant strain on Mary's marriage and her family's finances. Additionally, Nancy's drinking influence and stressful daily involvement in Mary's life affected Mary's drinking. Sometimes, Nancy encouraged Mary to drink with her. Other times, Nancy's behavior "drove" Mary to drink. Both scenarios negatively affect Mary's life. Despite the problems Nancy presented for Mary, she was proud of her ability to support her mother. Caring for her family was an integral part of Mary's sense of self. Actually, it was about all she had that was at least a little positive in her life.

Family of Creation

Because she was shy and overweight, as a young person Mary had no dating experience. That is, until she met her future husband John. John was an "overbearing" factory worker who began coming to the card shop "to talk." John easily flattered Mary because he was the first man ever to pay attention to her. Although he was 13 years older and difficult to get along with, Mary came to believe he was "the one." They were married less than six months after they met.

When we first met, Mary described her marriage as "rocky at best." John was frequently gone, spending less than half his nights at home. He did not participate in household and childcare responsibilities and often talked down to her, calling her "fat," "ugly," and "stupid." During the early years of their marriage, he hit her "a few times when he was drunk," but has not used physical violence regularly for more than 10 years. Mary refused to acknowledge any emotional abuse, sexual abuse, or power, and/or control issues in their marriage.

Mary and John had three children, John Jr., age 12, Jerry, age 11, and Jennifer, age six. John Jr., was a seventh grader who began playing football the year I met Mary. However, he recently quit the team. Although he was an above average student in elementary school, since beginning junior high his grades dropped significantly and he was frequently in trouble at school. Mary also said that John Jr. began treating her with contempt and disrespect in recent months. Mary believed that his anger pertained only to her drinking. She did not believe that John Jr. was angry with her for any other reasons.

Jerry, their middle child, was an honor roll student and active in school activities. He felt closest to his mother, frequently "standing up for her" against his father and brother. Sometimes, Jerry cared for Mary when she had a hangover.

The youngest, Jennifer, was a typical little girl who spent most of her time playing with dolls. Much like any six-year-old child, Jennifer "loved" both her parents and brothers. Overall, the relationship between the three siblings was typical of sibling interactions. They frequently "fussed" with each other, but mostly got along well.

Mary was the primary caretaker for the three children and I observed that she did a good job raising them. Mary refused to see her skills in that area. Raising her children correctly was important to Mary. She wanted to "do what's right" for her children and provide them the childhood that she "never had." Early on, Mary succeeded. During the first years of their lives, Mary was a good parent. However, in the last year parenting became progressively more difficult.

Impetus for Therapy

Mary believed her "real problems" began 11 months earlier. According to Mary, her troubles began on the day that John lost his job. John spent the first few months of unemployment looking for work, but struggled to find anything that paid what he made before. The longer he went without work, the more time he spent in the bars drinking until finally he stopped looking and kept drinking. A month after John's layoff, Mary's boss promoted her to full-time as an assistant manager. The new position provided the family with financial security and health insurance. However, it hurt John's pride to have his wife make more money than he did.

He began taking his wounded pride out on her verbally, physically, and sexually. The stress of unemployment and his wounded ego caused John to drink more and become more aggressive. He began going on weeklong drinking binges and spent little time at home. When he was home, he verbally assaulted Mary on numerous occasions and, for the first time in ten years, hit her.

Mary also said that he began "forcing himself" on her sexually in drunken rages. She hated him for doing this, but also said that he had his rights as her husband to have sex with her, even if it was forceful. Mary refused to define these events as rape. She did not believe that husbands could rape wives.

Questions

1. Examine the current literature on marital rape. What does current law and policy in your State say about this issue, and what recourse do victims of marital rape have in the legal system?

2. Examine the practice literature about the subject. What does the literature say about dealing with this issue in treatment? Was Mary's response about marital rape simply denial, or is this a common belief among clients in practice? How would you engage a client around this subject in practice?

Although Mary tried putting a positive spin on her marriage, by the time we met her relationship was deeply troubled. As a result, Mary's low mood symptoms increased, causing her to spend many nights self-medicating with food and alcohol. Her weight increased to over 250 pounds, further exacerbating her negative outlook. She drank to intoxication every night and began shirking her parental responsibilities. She also began having performance troubles at work.

A few months after John lost his job, the bank foreclosed on Nancy's home causing her to move in with Mary and her family. Drinking each day and night with her mother helped Mary realize that alcohol temporarily relieved her unhappiness. Between the alcohol, marital problems, and overall unhappiness, Mary's relationship with her children changed, particularly with her eldest son.

Before her DWI arrest, Mary began feeling that the contempt her son showed her related to her problems, specifically her drinking. Additionally, Mary began sensing that her work supervisor was not happy with her performance. On some level, Mary knew these problems related to her drinking. Hence, she said that she tried cutting down and stopping a few times. However, each attempt failed because Mary's home situation was not amenable to abstinence and she was not ready to make these significant changes in her life.

The Arrest

One morning while driving to work, the unthinkable happened. On the previous day, a particularly difficult day at work, Mary found the house "a mess" and her mother passed out on the sofa. She got into an argument with John Jr. that ended when she slapped him on the face for "cussing" at her.

Later that evening, Mary drank three bottles of wine. Waking up the next morning groggy and still drunk, Mary drove herself to work. On the way, she breezed through a red light. A police officer saw her run the light and pulled her over. Through routine questioning, the police officer smelled alcohol and arrested Mary for driving while intoxicated (DWI).

The arrest "shocked" Mary into reevaluating her life. While sitting in jail, she thought about her father's death, her mother's life, her messed up family, and her current troubles. Right then, Mary said that she decided to seek help.

Questions

The author presented background information and information pertaining to Mary's life and her presenting problem. Please respond to the following questions.

1. Based on the information presented above, construct a three-generation genogram and an eco-map that best represents Mary's involvement with multiple people, social systems, and organizations in her environment.
2. List the central issues in Mary's life at this moment, including supporting evidence. Include a list of the Mary's personal and environmental strengths that pertain to each of the issues you listed.
3. Develop a written multi-systemic assessment complete with diagnostic statement. Determine Mary's multi-axial (five axes and GAF scores) DSM diagnosis, or multiple diagnoses if indicated. Be sure that the information contained in your assessment defends your diagnostic decisions. It is not appropriate to base diagnostic decisions on assumptions, only direct evidence provided by your client. In addition, you may apply the PIE classification system to determine Mary's level of social functioning.
4. If you were to meet Mary, what additional information would you ascertain to contribute to a more holistic and comprehensive assessment?
5. Include whatever strengths Mary may have as central part of the assessment and diagnoses.

Mary's Diagnoses

Alcohol Abuse Symptoms

Mary met three of the four DSM-IV-TR criteria for substance abuse (APA, 2000). Her symptoms included continued drinking despite having (a) problems at work related to drinking, (b) interpersonal problems related to alcohol, and (c) being in hazardous situations while intoxicated (e.g. driving while intoxicated). Specifically, she reported having problems at work related to hangovers and trouble with her supervisor who suspected that she had a drinking problem. Mary also admitted to driving to work on a number of occasions with a hangover or still intoxicated from the day before. Additionally, she discussed frequent arguments with her husband and her oldest son while drinking. Additionally, Mary continued to drink despite the problems in these areas. Hence, she warranted the diagnosis of Alcohol Abuse. However, because Mary also met the criteria for Alcohol Dependence, I looked to that diagnosis for answers.

Alcohol Dependence Symptoms

In addition to meeting three of the four DSM criteria for alcohol abuse, Mary also met three of the seven DSM-IV-TR criteria for substance dependence (APA, 2000). Her symptoms included (a) increased tolerance marked by a need for increased amounts of alcohol to achieve the same effect and diminished effect with continued use, (b) use of larger than intended amounts over longer times than intended, and (c) a persistent desire yet inability to cut down and or quit. Therefore, I assigned Mary the diagnosis of alcohol dependence.

Dysthymia: Issues Co-Occurring with Mary's Alcoholism

Mary's Dysthymia-related symptoms and history of abuse became clear during the intakes assessment process. Despite her reports of drinking alcohol sporadically since age 22, Mary did not begin abusing alcohol until the past year when her family situation became more difficult. Mary's drinking fit the pattern of self-medication for co-occurring Dysthymia, relationship problems, low self-esteem, and abuse survivor.

Mary's inability to form and maintain healthy boundaries, especially related to her mother, further contributed to her drinking. These issues did not excuse her drinking, but shed light on important issues that needed addressing in the context of treatment. Dysthymia and low self-esteem (caused by childhood abuse, domestic violence, and marital rape) also became part of the treatment process to ensure success. Addressing these issues in the context of substance abuse treatment would help Mary eliminate some of the reasons for her drinking, therefore helping her achieve abstinence and prevent relapse.

Strength's Perspective

Using the strength's perspective helped me determine how to approach Mary's problems without further damaging her self-esteem by focusing only on the negative aspects of her life. The strength's perspective is "an orientation in social work and other professional practices that emphasizes the client's resources, capabilities, support systems and motivations to meet challenges and overcome adversity" (Barker, 1999, p. 468). It is important to note that this does not mean ignoring the existence of social problems and dysfunctions (Barker, 1999). Instead, using a strengths perspective emphasizes the client's assets in the process of identifying ways to help clients address their problems.

Apply the strength's perspective with Mary meant helping her to identify assets and strengths while linking these assets and strengths to ways she managed her life. Mary's primary strengths included her three children, a strong work ethic, a supportive work supervisor, personal organization, multiple personal achievements, and a spoken desire to become a good mother.

I carried a strengths-based approach throughout the treatment process, from assessment to termination. As our relationship developed, we built on her foundation of strengths by linking problem areas to current and past successes. Hence, change became easier and Mary could verbalize the changes she needed to make in her life without feeling hopeless about herself.

Education as Part of Therapy

An important part of clinical practice involves educating clients about healthy living (Granvold, 1994). Education involves providing information, modeling healthy behavior, and reinforcing healthy changes (Granvold, 1994). I introduced concepts of healthy living and provided education materials to help reinforce concepts introduced in our therapy (Granvold, 1994).

For example, during Mary's assessment, I introduced the concept of Alcohol Dependence by reviewing the diagnostic symptoms from the DSM-IV-TR with her based on the information she provided about her drinking (APA, 2000). As she came to understand her diagnosis and the need for abstinence, I provided written materials about the diagnosis for Mary to review at home. These materials offered alternative explanations of alcohol dependence and reinforced concepts addressed in session that Mary may have misunderstood or was too afraid to ask about during our first encounter.

I continued reinforcing these concepts throughout our relationship. I also employed the same process toward her other issues, including childhood abuse, domestic violence, healthy thinking, and Dysthymia. By teaching Mary about alcoholism, adult survivors of childhood abuse, and Dysthymia, she began seeing her problems differently and identifying a roadmap toward change.

Questions _____

1. Compare the assessment and diagnoses you developed with the author's assessment. What differences and similarities do you notice? What are the ramifications for treatment demonstrated by the differences between the two assessments?
2. Based on your assessment, now develop a written, treatment plan that includes short and long term treatment goals. Include what methods of treatment and support you will utilize and/or other levels of care that Mary might require.
3. Based on your assessment and treatment plan, what treatment theory, and/or combination of theories do you believe best fits Mary and her reality? Defend your decision.

Mary's Treatment Plan

I considered several factors regarding Mary's treatment plan. The first concerned Mary's ability and willingness to stop drinking and remain abstinent. Since she met the diagnostic criteria for alcohol dependence and she seemed most motivated to approach the subject, I decided to make abstinence her number one treatment goal.

Although Mary reported the motivation to stop drinking, she also agreed that sobriety might be difficult because of her unsupportive home environment. Both her mother and husband were active alcoholics who played a major role in Mary's drinking behavior. Moreover, her Dysthymic symptoms also influenced her drinking patterns, perhaps making her goal of abstinence more difficult to attain and maintain.

Secondly, I considered Mary's potential for physical withdrawal from alcohol. Clients who drink daily in the amount Mary reported have an increased likelihood of experiencing some degree of physical withdrawal symptoms (Schuckit, 1995). Hence, any treatment decision must first consider Mary's healthcare needs and the potential for health problems that can come from trying to stop drinking after long and heavy use.

Bringing Systems Together to Plan Treatment

As Mary's treatment plan began falling into place, I convened a Treatment Team Meeting to ensure that everyone involved in Mary's life agreed about her plans. Whenever possible, I call together all of the individuals involved in a client's life to discuss significant changes the client is attempting. By doing so, my client can feel supported by family members and other significant individuals in their lives while family members feel they are an important part of the change process. It also gives me the chance to assess any treatment needs others in the family might have because of my client's impending life changes.

Mary's treatment team included John, Nancy, her children, employer, and me. During the meeting, everyone including John and Nancy agreed that Mary should stop drinking. I then worked to ensure that Mary had the time and support to make her treatment program work. Hence, her supervisor gave her time-off and her family agreed to participate in therapy with Mary.

Mary's Primary Treatment Option

Focusing on sobriety was Mary's first treatment priority. As part of the planning process, we considered three levels of care available to people with substance related problems: (1) inpatient treatment or partial hospitalization, (2) intensive outpatient (sometimes referred to as day treatment or IOP), and (3) outpatient treatment. The level of care that is most appropriate for the client depends on a number of factors including risk for withdrawal, treatment acceptance, likelihood for continued use and recovery environment (American Society of Addictive Medicine (ASAM), 2001).

While a residential or inpatient treatment program offered the most restrictive and safe environment for Mary based on her drinking history and home environment, we had to consider the realities of her life in the treatment decision. Mary was the primary caretaker of three school-age children. Although her mother and husband could take care of the children, their own addictions made them unreliable. Mary said that leaving her children for two to four weeks was impossible. By considering Mary's personal and therapeutic needs in the context of the services available at each level of care, Mary decided that IOP was her best option.

Intensive Outpatient Programs (IOP)

Intensive outpatient treatment (IOP)—sometimes called day treatment—usually requires clients to check into a facility for several hours per day, allowing them to return home each night (Mooney, et al., 1992). IOP treatment primarily focuses on education, group, and individual therapy (Mooney, et al., 1992). IOP is similar to inpatient treatment, except clients continue to participate in their lives at home and work during treatment. Typically, clients appropriate for IOP are at a minimal risk for withdrawal, generally amenable to treatment but have some resistance, likely to continue using their drug of choice without close monitoring, and live in a difficult environment. However, clients appropriate for treatment at this level believe they can remain abstinent despite the lack of support in their home environment (ASAM, 2001).

The Second Chances Program

The two-week IOP called Second Chances was located 45 minutes from Mary's home and focused on confronting client denial systems and lifestyle change through individual therapy, group therapy, self-help groups, psycho-educational classes, and community interactions. A typical day included eight am check-in followed by community time and a 90-minute group. After group, clients participate in either Yoga or self-paced exercise followed by a 30-minute psychoeducational class and lunch. After lunch, they had individual therapy or free time with another psychoeducational class in the mid-afternoon. In addition to structured activities, clients participated in community activities and attended daily self-help groups such as Alcoholics Anonymous.

The program model provides clients the opportunity to learn how to live a substance free life in a community setting while still going home to live their "everyday life." The last two days of treatment include family activities designed to help family members understand the changes their loved one has made and the problems of adjusting to life after treatment.

Detoxification/Withdrawal Concerns

Detoxification and withdrawal were important considerations for Mary's treatment. Usually beginning 12 hours after the last drink and peaking at the 48 to 72 hour point, sudden withdrawal from alcohol can put the client's health at-risk (Schuckit, 1995). Symptoms of withdrawal include nervousness, shakiness, anxiety, irritability, emotional volatility, depression, fatigue, heart palpitations, headache, sweating, nausea, vomiting, insomnia, rapid heart rate, pupil dilation, clammy skin, hand and body tremors, and involuntary eyelid movements. At its worst, withdrawal can result in hallucinations, agitation, fever, convulsions, and stroke. Because of the health risks, clients with a high potential for withdrawal quit drinking under medical supervision (Schuckit, 1995).

Because Mary drank at least a bottle of wine every day, she had a high likelihood of experiencing withdrawal symptoms. For this reason, the clinic staff monitored Mary's progress during the first days of abstinence. As expected, Mary reported mild nervousness, depression, fatigue, and intense cravings in the first few days of abstinence. Fortunately, her symptoms were mild and dissipated within 72 hours. The Second Chances staff continued monitoring Mary daily for the entire time she was in the program.

Mary's IOP counselor reported that she was an exemplary patient who would graduate on time. However, Mary's counselor also noted concerns about her family and living situation. Although Mary made strides in the program, she would require a lot of support to maintain sobriety in a household with two active alcoholics. Regardless of concerns for her continued sobriety, Mary graduated from the program and returned to our clinic for aftercare to help her solidify the changes she made and help her progress further into recovery.

Sexual Abuse Revelations

As Mary became sober during IOP, she began experiencing terrifying nightmares, ultimately refusing to sleep. In concert with me, the IOP counselor confirmed my suspicion by suspecting herself that Mary had a history of sexual abuse. Slowly, Mary began revealing her past, that included sexual abuse by her alcoholic father and a neighbor who often looked after Mary and her brother while her parents drank. Each day, Mary would hint more towards this past, until finally in a group session, Mary "exploded."

As another female client discussed her sexual abuse as a child, Mary sat forward and said, "You think that's abuse? Hell, I would have gladly taken that. My father raped me everyday for two years . . . " Stunned, the group counselor referred Mary to her individual therapist to continue her revelations.

Mary reported that her father's abuse began slowly. At first, he would barge in on her while she showered or was changing her clothes. Then he began coming into her room at night and fondling her. Next, he forced her to fondle him. This led to him demanding oral sex and finally forced intercourse. The abuse went on daily for nearly three years until his accidental death.

Simultaneously, a male neighbor ("Uncle Jim") forced Mary to perform oral sex for him when he babysat Mary and her brother while her parents were out drinking on weekends. She said that this lasted for over two years, and occurred most every weekend.

Mary said that over the years she "forgot" about the sexual abuse, because it did not help her to think about it. She never tried telling her mother, who, according to Mary, "had her own problems to deal with." After her father's death, she decided that she could not burden anyone with her problems because the family had it rough enough. Over time, Mary just assumed that "these things happened to all girls," and simply pushed the memories deep into her psyche. Certainly, this day was a milestone in Mary's treatment and impending recovery.

Follow-up Treatment (Aftercare)

After completing IOP, Mary began aftercare with me at the clinic. Lasting for as long as the client needs to remain sober, aftercare helps ease clients back into the "real world" while maintaining the progress they made in the more intensive treatment programs (Mooney, et al., 1992). Services included in aftercare depend on individual needs and typically include individual therapy, group counseling, education, and/or support groups such as Alcoholics Anonymous (AA) or Rational Recovery (Mooney, et al., 1992). Because she had multiple layers of problems, Mary also needed mental health support in addition to addictions-related aftercare services.

In our first session after IOP, Mary and I discussed her needs for aftercare. We agreed to include individual therapy, a female sexual abuse survivor's support group, and an addictions recovery support group to help her deal with alcoholism, childhood abuse issues, Dysthymia, obesity, and marital problems. By developing a program that addressed Mary's various problems, I hoped that she would successfully negotiate the stages of recovery by dealing with the co-occurring issues contributed to her drinking behavior in the first place.

Stages of Recovery

In substance abuse treatment, there are three conceptual stages of recovery clients must navigate for success: stabilization, rehabilitation, and maintenance (Smyth, 1996). In the stabilization stage, clients become abstinent, accept that they have problems with alcohol (or drugs), and make a commitment to change (Smyth, 1996). In the rehabilitation stage, treatment focuses on helping clients establish alcohol free lifestyles and alcohol free identities. The maintenance stage focuses on solidifying gains made in treatment, preventing relapse, and preparing for termination (Smyth, 1996).

Mary entered aftercare in the maintenance stage. Maintenance is often the most difficult stage because it requires clients to maintain sobriety and other personal changes despite daily pressures from life. The two alcoholics she lived with at home impeded Mary's progress in this stage. I focused on helping Mary deal with these negative influences while also improving self esteem, coping skills, and healthy boundaries. I accomplished these goals by having Mary participate in an alcohol recovery group (self-help), a sexual abuse survivors group, and individual therapy.

Self-Help Groups

Mary agreed to attend a self-help recovery group. Although a number of options were available, Mary chose Alcoholics Anonymous (AA). AA is a self-help organization designed to help people who have alcohol related problems (i.e., are alcoholics) stop drinking (Alcoholics Anonymous World Services (AA), 2000). An all-voluntary organization of recovering people, AA uses a 12-step recovery process (AA).

At first, Mary felt "weird" at AA meetings. With my encouragement, Mary stuck it out for a few weeks and, as many clients do, grew to like it. Working the 12-steps of AA helped Mary accept her problems with alcohol and food. Because she felt comfortable working the 12-step process, she carried the process over to the work she did in the sexual abuse survivors group and individual therapy.

Sexual Abuse Survivors Group

Mary also agreed to attend a women's only sexual abuse survivors group. Commonly used as a tool in the treatment of survivors of domestic violence and childhood abuse (Corey & Corey, 1997; Paleg & Jongsma, 2000), the survivors group provided Mary a supportive environment to confront the memories and lingering symptoms of her sexual abuse and to help develop healthy strategies for living. Group work, whether in a support group or therapy group format, is an important component in the treatment of female survivors of sexual abuse and domestic violence (Corey & Corey; Paleg & Jongsma).

Mary's survivors group met during her lunch break and became a valuable place for her to develop relationships with other women with similar backgrounds and lives. In this group, Mary saw how her marriage and the relationship with her mother were abusive and harmful to her and her children. After a while in group, Mary decided to change her relationships and work to develop healthy relations with other people.

Individual Therapy

During individual therapy, Mary combined her survivor issues, treatment for Dysthymia, and her overeating with components of alcohol recovery. I employed a cognitive behavioral approach to help Mary work through the 12-steps of recovery (AA, 2000) while also addressing her underlying issues of Dysthymia, low self-esteem, and problems with interpersonal boundaries.

Cognitive-behavioral therapy tends to be short term, focused on the present, and addresses specific goals (Granvold, 1994). Defined as "approaches to treatment using selected concepts and techniques from behaviorism, social learning theory, action therapy, functional school of social work, task centered treatment and therapies based on cognitive models" (Barker, 1999, p. 84), cognitive-behavioral interventions are excellent tools to help clients reduce presenting symptoms. It is also an effective treatment model for mood disorders (Granvold, 1994).

As Mary and I worked through her issues, she became motivated to process through painful childhood memories of sexual abuse to reduce her symptoms and facilitate change. As a result, I introduced introspective, insight-oriented treatment techniques into Mary's regime. Insight therapies are "treatment approaches oriented toward helping individuals achieve greater self-awareness and understanding of their conscious and unconscious motivations, emotions, thought processes, and underlying reasons for behavior" (Barker, 1999, p. 243). Although we primarily focused on behavior change in the here-and-now, we used several sessions for Mary to work through hurtful childhood memories.

Using Genograms in Practice

To help Mary identify and understand how intergenerational addictions, domestic violence, and sexual abuse affected her life, together we drew a genogram of her family.

Famous family therapist Murray Bowen introduced genograms to clinical practice to depict family relationships over at least three generations (Bowen, 1980; Kramer, 1985; McGoldrick, Gerson, & Shellenberger, 1999). We completed Mary's genogram over two sessions. By looking at her family graphically, Mary realized that addiction, domestic violence, and sexual abuse ran throughout her family. The awareness depicted by Mary viewing her family in graphic form motivated her to make changes to stop the abuse in her generation.

Questions

Now that the author has discussed the treatment plan she developed for Mary, compare the treatment plan used in the case with the treatment plan you developed for Mary earlier.
1. **In what ways does your treatment plan differ from the authors? Please develop an informed critique of the authors plan, and include the reasons you agree or disagree with the author's choices.**
2. **What do the differences between treatment plans imply for treatment in this case?**

Compelling Issues in Treatment

Mary's case presented three compelling issues for consideration in treatment: (1) Dependence versus codependence, (2) Multigenerational patterns of violence and sexual abuse, and (3) Obesity. Addressing these areas was critical in Mary's life and treatment.

Dependence versus Codependence

Dependence is, "a state of reliance on other people or things for existence or support" (Barker, 1999, p. 123). Codependence is defined as "the relationship between two or more people who rely on each other to meet and provide for reciprocal needs, particularly unhealthy ones" (Barker, 1999, p. 84). Mary confronted both issues.

When we first met, Mary was dependant on alcohol and food as her primary coping mechanisms. When problems exacerbated, Mary ate and drank excessively. Likewise, both her mother Nancy and her husband John were dependant on alcohol and Mary for support. Mary enabled each to continue with their respective addictions by not holding them accountable for their actions or responsible for appropriate contributions to the family. In this way, Mary developed codependent relationships with John and Nancy that contributed to her felt need for alcohol and overeating. Systemically, John and Nancy enabled Mary's addictive behaviors as well. The family became a "support" network for self-destructive behaviors.

Mary's dependency on food and alcohol and co-dependent relationships with John and Nancy fed each other, making her treatment difficult and complicated.

Because Mary's co-dependency issues fed her dependency issues, we decided to begin treatment with Mary's food and alcohol addictions. As is often the case, getting sober was the easy part of treatment. Remaining sober required further work. That is, for Mary to remain sober, she had to address the boundary problems inherent in codependent relationships.

Unfortunately, over time these moves caused significant change in her life. Systemically, as Mary changed so did her environment and those closest to her. In time, her marriage dissolved and her relationship with Nancy grew strained. She walked the tightrope most recovering people must walk between maintaining the status quo and change. In Mary's case, change in her life meant change for everyone involved.

Intergenerational Transmission of Abuse and Violence

A second set of issues involved the power of intergenerational transmission of abuse and violence in Mary's family. People raised in domestically violent and sexually abusing families are at a greater risk for experiencing both as adults (Alexander & Warner, 2003; Ehrensaft, Cohen, & Brown, 2003; Kwong, Bartholomew, & Henderson, 2003). Children exposed to domestic violence and sexual abuse has their mental models of intimate relationships skewed, making them more susceptible to use violence and/or become the victim of violence in intimate relationships (Alexander & Warner, 2003). Additionally, abused children (sexual or violently) develop insecure attachment strategies making adult intimate relationships difficult, at best (Alexander & Warner, 2003).

In my work with Mary, we used genograms to help her understand her family's intergenerational patterns of abuse and violence. Mary saw how being raised in a domestically violent and sexually abusive family carried through to her marriage and family. Her husband abused her sexually (rape) and violently over the years. Mary's mental model learned in childhood allowed her to accept the abuse as if it was something "everyone" experienced.

Understanding how the intergenerational transmission of abuse and violence affects client's lives can help practitioners develop effective strategies for ending the abusive cycles in their lives (Alexander, & Warner, 2003). By understanding her family history of abuse and violence, Mary ended the patterns and form healthy relationships.

Obesity

It is important that practitioners be aware of the oppression and cultural stereotypes their overweight and obese clients face. Negative stereotypes related to body size are as devastating as other negative and hostile cultural stereotypes such as race, gender, and sexual orientation. Practitioners working with overweight and obese clients must address these issues while promoting overall health over thinness, and help clients become self-accepting instead of self-depriving through strict diets (Connors, & Melcher, 1993).

I believe that helping clients address the reasons behind their unhealthy lifestyle leads them to begin making healthier choices. Mary's obesity was a manifestation of other problems in her life. Therefore, we did not focus on reducing her weight as a primary goal in treatment. Instead, we focused on resolving her drinking problems, developing healthy relationships, and improving her self-image. As her lifestyle and self-image improved, she lost weight—with no dieting required.

Questions

The author addressed three compelling issues to consider in treatment with Mary. Before moving on in the case, are there other compelling issues that you believe must be included in this discussion? If so, explain the issues and discuss the reasons you believe make them important to the case.

Ethical Considerations

In Mary's case I addressed two primary ethical issues that affected my decision making process. The first issue related to domestic violence and marital rape early in treatment. I decided early in our relationship to allow her domestic violence issues, including her reports of marital rape, to take a back seat to working on her alcohol addiction and mental health concerns.

I had two reasons for this strategy. Firstly, I believe it is impossible to treat mental health or domestic violence/sexual abuse issues when clients have active substance dependence problems. I approach clients with co-occurring disorders from the perspective that alcohol (or other drug) masks all other problems, making it impossible to separate these other problems from the addictions. For example, when Mary drank it was impossible to know how much of her baseline low mood was a result of Dysthymia and how much was a result of alcohol.

Secondly, I targeted her drinking first, her mental health concerns second and the domestic violence/abuse third because Mary did not realize that she lived in an abusive environment. She wanted to address her drinking. At some level, I am sure that Mary knew she lived in harmful circumstances, but she had trouble coming to terms with the idea that they were abusive, primarily because the abuse had lessened recently and her family always treated her that way. She came to treatment not realizing that her life could be different in this way—that abuse was not normal or acceptable. This realization only came after sobriety and through ongoing work and support from her survivors group.

By focusing on her presenting problems (alcohol dependence and Dysthymia), Mary linked these issues to her abusive past and present. That is, Mary came to terms with her victimization in her own time, when she was ready to address the issues. I decided that since her life was not in jeopardy that working on the domestic violence issues later was appropriate in Mary's case. I may have handled another case differently, depending on the unique dynamics of that case.

I did not ignore the issue, but monitored it throughout early treatment. Had there been evidence that the abuse continued or became potentially harmful or lethal, I would have taken a more an aggressive approach immediately. I believe that addressing the alcohol dependence first, Dysthymia second, and abuse third was an example of starting where the client was and working from there, a component of skillful social work practice (Shulman, 1999).

Self Determination and Consequences

My second ethical concern related to Mary suffering the consequences of her actions. Watching our clients regularly make poor decision can be difficult for practitioners. Many practitioners feel the urge to "catch" clients as they fall with the thought that it will soften the hurt they feel. Particularly with substance abusing clients, I believe it is important to resist this urge, instead allowing clients to live the consequences of their own actions (Mooney, et al., 1992).

Allowing them to find their own "bottom" sometimes means backing away and letting clients make decisions that practitioners know are harmful (Mooney, et al., 1992). Often, the act of hitting rock bottom provides insight into their problems that promote change in their lives. However, this means allowing clients to walk in harm's way. It is important to remember that when adults can make their own decisions. Therefore, the harm that may come because of client's decisions is their choice, not the practitioners.

On numerous occasions with Mary, I had to step back and allow her to make poor decisions in her life. For example, it was difficult to hear Mary tell me about her poor marriage that included abuse. Although we addressed issues related to power and control, self-respect, and threats to sobriety, it was Mary's decision to remain married or leave. She decided to stay in the marriage for several months. I respected her decision, allowing her to suffer the consequences of her decision. When she was ready to make changes, I supported her decision. My goal was to be there for her to help her stand up again after a fall, not to stop her from falling. Change takes time. For Mary, change took a long time. However, she learned from her mistakes and was able to change her life when she was ready.

Questions

The author presented two ethical issues she considered in this case: delaying treatment for abuse and the client's right to self determination. Before moving on, consider the following.

1. **What is your opinion of the author's presentation of the issues? Examine the code of professional ethics in your profession and the current practice literature regarding these subjects. What could the author have done differently? What would you do differently if you worked with a client such as Mary?**

2. **What other potential ethical issues were presented in this case? Explain the issues and explicate how you would address whatever ethical issues you discover in this case.**

From Change to Termination

Helping clients make lasting change takes time and patience, especially clients such as Mary who present with multiple, serious problems. Over the course of our relationship, Mary discovered that confronting layers of hurt, developing new ways of acting, and finding healthy relationships was difficult. Although successful in the two-week IOP and the first weeks of aftercare, Mary ran into trouble in aftercare. Her family relationships, personal fear, combined with the dilemma of change led Mary on a roller coaster of emotions, relapses, and recoveries that lasted more than two years. I expected her to drop out of treatment altogether. However, her tenacity prevailed and she stuck with it.

Time and Patience

Mary's first drinking relapse came after 61 days of sobriety. The night before, Mary left her AA meeting "feeling great." She called me to say how "awesome" it felt to "have done it." She was proud of her accomplishments to date. She attended AA and her survivor's group regularly, established healthier boundaries with her mother, improving at work, exercising, eating right, and improving her relationship with the children. The next day, Mary and her mother "got into it, big time." Mary described their fight as "the worst we ever had," leaving Mary exhausted, hurt, and tired.

A few hours later, Mary drank a bottle of strawberry wine, fell asleep, and regretted it the next day. During the next weeks of therapy, Mary was forthcoming about her relapse in all aspects of treatment. She wanted to "redeem" herself and make amends to her family, her sponsor, and herself. I worked with her to understand why she drank. We focused on her history of self- defeating behaviors and self-sabotage. Although Mary said that she understood why she drank and made a new commitment to sobriety, this was only the first of many problems she experienced during treatment.

Three weeks later, Mary stopped attending individual therapy and her groups. For more than a month, she avoided all aspects of therapy including AA and the friends she made in the survivor's group. I tried contacting her during the month-long hiatus. However, she did not return my calls or respond to the letter I sent. I believed she had left treatment for good.

However, one member of her survivor's group took matters into her own hands. Noting Mary's repeated absence from survivors group, this member went to Mary's home and convinced her to return to group. At the survivors group, members talked her into returning to AA and individual therapy. After a short period, Mary reestablished her sobriety and began making other strides in her life again.

Once back in therapy, Mary revealed that her personal life had changed significantly. Just before she stopped therapy, John told her that he was having an affair and intended to continue seeing his new lover. Mary stated that John did not want a divorce; he just wanted to see other people. Although by then Mary could see how unhealthy her marriage was, she still loved John and did not want the marriage to end.

To cope with the grief of her husband's affair, Mary turned back to food and alcohol for self-medication. This spiraled into a cycle of guilt over her relapse leading to more drinking and eating to cope with the guilt. From the guilt about her actions and fear of moral judgment by me and her friends in group, Mary refused to return for help. Using the strengths perspective, I helped Mary see that people did not judge her actions and that all relapses—while difficult—can teach people valuable lessons about themselves.

Over the next two years, Mary faced many personal challenges including deciding to pursue a divorce, changing the relationship with Nancy, and returning to night school to finish her high school diploma. Although these challenges were difficult, Mary continued in therapy. Her tenacity, the support of the survivor's group, and AA helped her to progress in her treatment. Ultimately, she weighed less than 200 pounds, exercised regularly, received a promotion at work, developed healthier relationships with her family, and met a "nice man" through friends.

Termination

Therapy is supposed to be temporary. Hence, practitioners must help clients understand that their therapeutic relationship will eventually end (Shulman, 1999). For this reason, preparing for termination begins during the first session (Shulman, 1999). While Mary spent most of two years in treatment, her therapy also needed to end.

I began the termination process by gradually reducing our frequency of contact. At first, Mary attended weekly individual therapy, weekly survivor's group, and AA "every other day." As Mary improved, I reduced individual therapy to bi- weekly, returning to weekly sessions when Mary fell into crisis. Mary's attendance at AA and survivor's group continued at the same frequency.

After Mary achieved six months of stability (23 months of treatment), we began discussing termination. During the last session, we reviewed her progress and planned for potential problems in the future. As we said goodbye, I reminded Mary that she could return anytime she felt it necessary.

Wrapping Things Up

Mary demonstrated many problems that practitioners find with persons with co-occurring disorders, including alcoholism, Dysthymia, childhood sexual abuse, and domestic violence. By starting with Mary's presenting problem of alcohol dependence, we wove together services to address her other problems in therapy. By learning about Mary and other clients like her, practitioners can learn about how they will handle similar situations.

A Few Years Later . . .

A few years after termination, Mary continued to attend AA and the survivors group. Being a seasoned veteran of both groups, Mary has taken leadership roles including becoming a sponsor for a young woman much like herself who struggles with alcoholism and abuse-related issues. She married the "nice man" she met in her second year of therapy, finished high school, and was taking business courses at the local college.

Her relationship with Nancy remained tenuous, but healthier than ever. Her children were happy, doing well in school, and proud of their mom. In fact, John Jr. planned to attend college and received a partial academic scholarship. Overall, Mary was a success story that can teach us about practice issues we find with many of our clients.

Questions

The author presented an interesting, successfully terminated case that involved many issue commonly found in practice with sexual abuse cases. Taking a broad view of this case, reevaluate the author's work and your participation through the questions asked throughout the case.

1. Review Mary's progress in treatment. Based on the author's description, the professional literature, and the latest practice evidence, what occurred to account for Mary's progress?
2. What was the theoretical approach or combination of approaches that appeared to work best for Mary?
3. What additional intervention(s) would you recommend? Use the professional literature and latest practice evidence to justify your recommendations.
4. Overall, what is your professional opinion of the work performed in this case? As always, refer to the professional literature, practice evidence, your experience, and the experience of peers when developing your opinion.
5. Based on your review, what additional or alternative approaches could the author have used with Mary? That is, if you were the practitioner, how would you have approached this case? Please explain and justify your approach.
6. What did the case demonstrate that you could use in other practice settings? List the most important issues you learned and their relevance in your future practice career.

Bibliography

Alcoholics Anonymous World Services. (2000). *Alcoholic's anonymous* (4th ed.). New York, NY: Author.

Alexander, P. C., & Warner, S. (2003). Attachment theory and family systems theory as frameworks for understanding the intergenerational transmission of family violence. In P. Erdman, & T. Caffery (Eds.), *Attachment and family systems: Conceptual, empirical, and therapeutic relatedness* (pp. 241–257), New York, NY: Brunner-Routledge.

American Psychiatric Association. (2000). *Diagnostic and statistics manual of mental disorders* (4th ed.). Washington, DC: Author.

American Society of Addiction Medicine. (2001). *Patient placement criteria* (2nd ed.). Chevy Chase, MD: Author.

Barker, R. L. (1999). *The social work dictionary*. Washington, DC: NASW Press.

Bowen, M. (1980). Key to the use of the genogram. In E. A. Carter. & M. McGoldrick (Eds.), *The family life cycle: A framework for family therapy*. New York: Gardner.

Connors, M. E., & Melcher, S. A. (1993). Ethical issues in the treatment of weight-dissatisfied clients. *Professional psychology, 24*(4), 404–408.

Corey, M. S., & Corey, G. (1997). *Groups: Process and practice* (5th ed.). Belmont, CA: Brooks/Cole Publishing.

Ehrensaft, M. K., Cohen, P., & Brown, J. (2003). Intergenerational transmission of partner violence: A 20-year prospective study. *Journal of Consulting and Clinical Psychology, 71*(4), 741–753.

Granvold, D. K. (1994). *Cognitive and behavioral treatment: Methods and applications*. Pacific Grove, CA: Brooks/Cole Publishing.

Johnson, J. L. (2004). *Fundamentals of substance abuse practice*. Pacific Grove, CA: Brooks/Cole.

Kwong, M. J., Bartholomew, K., & Henderson, A. J. Z. (2003). The intergenerational transmission of relationship violence. *Journal of Family Psychology, 17*(3), 288–301.

Mooney, A. J., Eisenberg, A., & Eisenberg, H. (1992). *The recovery workbook*. New York: Workman Publishing Company.

McGoldrick, M., Gerson, R., & Shellenberger, S. (1999). *Genograms: Assessment and intervention* (2nd ed.), New York: W.W. Norton & Company.

Paleg, K., & Jongsma, A. E. (2000). *The group therapy treatment planner*. New York: Wiley.

Payne, M. S. (1997). *Modern social work theory, second edition*. Chicago, IL: Lyceum Books.

Schuckit, M. A. (1995). *Drug and alcohol abuse: A clinical guide to diagnosis and treatment* (4th ed.). New York: Plenum Medical Book Company.

Shulman, L. (1999). *The skills of helping individuals, families, groups, and communities* (4th ed.). Itasca, IL: F. E. Peacock Publishers.

Smyth, N. J. (1996). Substance abuse: Direct practice. In Beebe, L., Winchester, N. A., Pflieger, F., & Lowman, S. (Eds.), *Encyclopedia of Social Work* (pp. 2328–2338). Washington, DC: NASW Press.

Turner, F. J. (1996). Social Work Practice: Theoretical Base. In Beebe, L., Winchester, N. A., Pflieger, F., & Lowman, S. (Eds.), *Encyclopedia of Social Work* (pp. 2258–2265). Washington, DC: NASW Press.